Michael Molkentin

FLYING THE SOUTHERN CROSS

Aviators Charles Ulm and Charles Kingsford Smith

NATIONAL LIBRARY OF AUSTRALIA

NATIONAL
LIBRARY
OF AUSTRALIA

Published by the National Library of Australia
Canberra   ACT   2600
© National Library of Australia 2012
Reprinted 2012

Text © Michael Molkentin
Foreword © John Ulm

Books published by the National Library of Australia further the Library's objectives to interpret
and highlight the Library's collections and to support the creative work of the nation's writers and
researchers.

National Library of Australia Cataloguing-in-Publication entry

Author: Molkentin, Michael.
Title: Flying the Southern Cross : Charles Ulm and Charles Kingsford Smith /
                 Michael Molkentin.
ISBN: 9780642277466 (pbk.)
Notes: Includes bibliographical references and index.
Subjects: Ulm, C. T. P. (Charles Thomas Phillippe), 1897–1934.
                 Kingsford-Smith, Charles, Sir, 1897–1935.
                 Southern Cross (Airplane)
                 Transpacific flights.
Dewey Number: 629.13092
Commissioning Publisher: Susan Hall
Publisher's Editor: John Mapps
Production coordinator: Melissa Bush
Image coordinators: Felicity Harmey and Gina Wyatt
Special photography: Digitisation and Photography Branch, National Library of Australia
Designer: Elizabeth Faul
Printed and bound in Singapore by Imago
Cover image: see pages 129 and 157

CONTENTS

FOREWORD

John Ulm, 14 years old in 1935 with Charles Kingsford Smith.

My earliest recollection of my father Charles Ulm dates to a few days after he completed the trans-Pacific flight in June 1928, when he came to my new home where I was living with my mother and stepfather—bringing a Hornby train set for my seventh birthday.

In his final six years I was with him for odd weekends, maybe a total of ten days.

His newly appointed secretary Ellen Rogers happened to live in the next street. By arrangement she would pick up little Johnny— steam train to the Quay ferry, tram to Martin Place, and his Australian National Airways CEO's office in Challis House. Then in the tiny black Triumph with 'Rog' and a typewriter in the dicky seat to his Dover Heights bungalow where with his big Zeiss binoculars I would watch the great Sydney Harbour Bridge's arches edging together.

I recall a day on his yacht with him holding me by shorts and shirt over the side for fun; and being ordered below by Captain Ulm when she heeled over defying the Southerly Buster. He explained how wind suction over sails led to the design of aeroplane wings.

School friends asked whether my dad was going to fly in the 1934 London–Melbourne Air Race. He wrote saying no, because he was planning his survey flight for the first regular trans-Pacific airmail services. When he was lost, strangers touched me in the street. They knew who the little boy was. It brought it all in on me.

In 1935 (his own last year) Smithy kindly had me in my father's pilot seat alongside him for the last flight of the *Southern Cross*—me wearing my father's trans-Pacific flying helmet and waving proudly to my school assembled below.

It was after flying in my own war, and with a career developing aviation journalism and Australian international airline expansion, that I came fully to appreciate the centrality of my family name and my father's towering stature in our aviation history, attested by contemporaries and historians.

Loyal to her last day, 'Rog' collated the records which we lodged in the libraries: the 'Charles T.P. Ulm Collection'. Papers and memorabilia keep coming in to me, though, the latest being his last cabled message to *The Sun* from Fiji before taking off for Brisbane and triumph.

The Pacific flight raised the eyes of a distant, insular Australia to a world now brought near. Today, a million Australians live and prosper abroad, and we catch planes like buses.

Technical record that it is, my father's log is about four people: Charles Kingsford Smith and his flying skills, Charles Ulm and his organising ability, and the vital Americans, radioman Jim Warner and navigator Harry Lyon. (Many years later, Harry confided to me: 'The latest model drift recorder Charlie Ulm had acquired for me was so awkward to hold out the little door to take readings that I threw the goddamn thing into the Pacific'. His dead reckoning saved them all.)

Michael Molkentin has mined the lode from this 'stuff of history', uncovering the character of the cast members—their personalities, pluses and minuses, strengths and weaknesses, foibles and failings.

With exacting research, insight and historical integrity he has masterfully crafted his gripping account of Australian achievement. It will sit well with the treasures carefully tended in our pillared National Library, itself Australia's richest treasure.

John Ulm

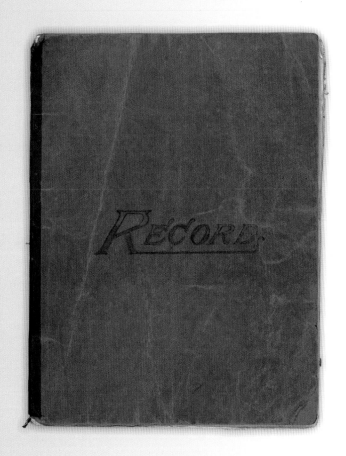

AUTHOR'S NOTE

Each chapter in this book begins with an extract from Charles Ulm's log presented as a facsimile page from the original document, together with a transcription.

Ulm's log has previously been published on two occasions. In 1928, during the trans-Pacific flight, Sydney newspaper *The Sun* carried extracts from the log. Later that year, an account of the flight ghost-written by journalist Hugh Buggy, *The Story of the Southern Cross Trans-Pacific Flight 1928*, also included a transcribed version of Ulm's log. In both cases Ulm's words were edited to varying degrees (and at times extensively). In this book transcripts of the log appear for the first time unedited from the original document, held in the National Library of Australia's Charles Kingsford Smith papers (MS 209, Item 1). The entries are transcribed without corrections to spelling, grammar or punctuation.

The National Library has digitised the log and made it freely available online at http://www.nla.gov.au/apps/cdview?pi=nla.ms-ms209-1.

Curiously, three pages are missing from the original log, containing, it appears, entries describing *Southern Cross'* arrival in Honolulu, Suva and Brisbane. There is no trace of when and how these pages were separated from the original. However the versions published in 1928 contain these now-missing extracts, allowing us to fill these gaps in the original document's chronology.

The crew of *Southern Cross* described their experiences in various memoirs, articles and interviews. These are quoted freely throughout the narrative, though quotations from Ulm's log are always attributed as such. A full list of references for quotations from other sources is available at http://publishing.nla.gov.au/refs or www.michaelmolkentin.com.

Throughout the flight, Ulm recorded time based on the time zone of their point of take-off. Occasionally he noted the time at their current location but prefaced this as 'ship's time'. The initials 'PCT' in the log stand for Pacific Coast Time.

For clarity, measurements in the chapter text are converted to metric values with the exception of altitude, which remains in feet, as it does in modern aviation vernacular.

'NOTES WRITTEN ABOVE THE CLOUDS'

Charles Ulm's log and the 1928 trans-Pacific flight

Charles Ulm and Charles Kingsford Smith enjoying their new-found celebrity in the immediate aftermath of the trans-Pacific flight. An honorary commission in the Royal Australian Air Force was but one of many rewards from a besotted nation.

At 13 minutes past ten, on the chilly Saturday morning of 9 June 1928, a blue and silver Fokker monoplane named *Southern Cross* touched down on the grass airstrip of Eagle Farm aerodrome, just outside Brisbane. There to witness it a crowd of some 15,000 spectators had gathered, eager to experience a moment of monumental historical gravity.

The aeroplane and its crew, Charles Kingsford Smith, Charles Ulm, Jim Warner and Harry Lyon, had just completed the first flight across the Pacific. In nine days, these four men covered the 11,917 kilometres from San Francisco to Brisbane in an aircraft constructed largely of timber and fabric. The two Australian organisers of the venture, Kingsford Smith and Ulm, were at this triumphant moment, world famous, each on the threshold of a remarkable career in pioneering aviation.

Southern Cross came to a stop amid a scene of unbridled chaos. The crowd surged forward to glimpse the aviators whose epic journey they had been following in the press for the last week and a half. Throughout the flight Ulm had recorded an almost-constant stream of notes in a logbook to cable to Sydney's daily newspaper *The Sun* at the end of each leg. Also, his regular wireless messages from the aircraft had been broadcast live by radio stations into Australia's lounge rooms. This clever use of the press, conceived by Ulm, involved ordinary Australians, isolated from world events, in a way they never had been before. Indeed, by the

'Heroes of the First Trans-Pacific Flight'

time they reached Brisbane, Ulm's brown notebook—his 'log'—was almost as famous as he and his companions.

While the police battled to keep the crowds at bay, Kingsford Smith and Ulm climbed down from the open sides of *Southern Cross*' cockpit to be greeted by officials. There and then, amid the din of cheering, the federal government's Controller of Civil Aviation, on instructions from the Prime Minister, asked Ulm if he would be willing to donate his log to the Commonwealth 'so that the record of the flight could be preserved for future generations'. Ulm agreed immediately and over the following days the fact became public to widespread acclaim

Though partners in a joint venture, Kingsford Smith (left) and Ulm (right) have received uneven public esteem, both then and now.

in the press. *The Sun* declared the log a priceless document of Australian history, describing it as 'written surely under the strangest imaginable conditions—staccato notes jotted down as the *Southern Cross* tossed and dived in the fury of the storm: notes written above the clouds at 6000 feet; notes written when the ocean was but a few hundred feet below'.

This was not just idle sentiment from one of the flight's financial backers. When the Parliamentary Library—from which the National Library of Australia developed— accepted the log into its collection in November 1928, the Speaker of the House of Representatives declared it 'one of our most interesting and treasured items' and arranged for its permanent display in Parliament House.

Today, Ulm's 'staccato notes' are preserved in the National Library of Australia, along with a voluminous amount of published and archival material relating to the flight. Indeed, the event must rate among the most comprehensively documented in Australian history; an indication of the significance attributed to it by both its contemporaries and generations since. Yet amid hundreds of photographs, private and official correspondence, manuscripts, maps and even the notes used by the crew to communicate during the 82 hours they spent in the air, Ulm's log stands out as a particularly valuable record.

On its lined pages Ulm captured, in a hand often unsteadied by turbulence, a unique and authentic sense of the moment. It is not a

The Sun initially credited the log extracts to 'Captain Kingsford Smith', obscuring Ulm's part in the flight.

polished journal written retrospectively after reflection. Ulm's terse, methodically time-logged entries record his raw impressions as they came to him during the flight. They are rough and incisive—'unliterary in essence' as one newspaper editor described them—but therein lies their immediacy and striking sense of authenticity.

The importance of Ulm's log as a historical document is that it also casts light on the origins of the Kingsford Smith 'legend'. Although the log was written by Ulm and painstakingly transmitted by him in Morse code following each exhausting leg of the journey, the newspapers used it, somewhat ironically, to highlight Kingsford Smith's role. Indeed, when *The Sun* reproduced Ulm's accounts, it promoted them as an 'exclusive' from 'Captain Kingsford Smith's diary' and changed the personal pronouns to suggest that he had written the entries. Although the precise reasons behind this are unclear, it seems likely there was a deliberate editorial decision to give Kingsford Smith— the flight's chief pilot—the narrative's focus. Whatever the reason, the results have resonated. In the 1950s, Ulm's son John found his father's log displayed in the Parliament House foyer labelled as 'Kingsford Smith's diary'. After some 'gentle ribbing', recalls Ulm, the Parliamentary Librarian Sir Harold White—an old friend of his—apologetically corrected the oversight. The log, however, remained part of the Kingsford Smith papers, as it does to this day in the National Library's collection.

Although a party to the creation of the 'Smithy' legend, the log also sheds light on Ulm's contribution to the flight as its organiser and co-pilot for about a third of the flying hours. It provides a useful counterbalance to Kingsford Smith's immense historical weight, suggesting that, contrary to popular belief, there were others of significant talent and dedication behind the man Australians proclaimed 'the world's greatest aviator'.

Kingsford Smith himself well knew that he flew as part of a team. We are the ones responsible for any distortions in the history of his achievements, not 'Smithy'. Kingsford Smith regularly deprecated the press' attention and emphasised the contribution made by his colleagues. As he declared on radio station 2BL after landing in Sydney, 'this flight was not my flight'.

> It was a flight by Charles Ulm, Harry Lyon, Jim Warner and the chap that's talking to you. None could have succeeded without the others. Each man had his own specialised job. And the fact that each man did do his job accounts for our presence here in Australia.

Using Ulm's log alongside the rest of the National Library's rich array of sources, this book attempts to explain just how, indeed, these four men and their timber and fabric aircraft managed to do it.

Two young men fascinated by flight

Charles Edward Smith—the family added 'Kingsford' later—began life in Brisbane on 9 February 1897, seventh child of Catherine and William Smith. The following year, Charles Thomas Phillippe Ulm was born in Melbourne, third son of Emile Gustave Ulm, a French migrant and his Australian wife, Ada. The first aircraft were yet to fly; indeed, Smith would be almost seven years old before the newspapers reported the Wright brothers' first flight. Still, these boys started life in an era of remarkable change. Machines and science were transforming the lives of ordinary people, evoking both anxiety and optimism as the twentieth century dawned.

When they were still young, both boys' families settled in Sydney's North Shore. Ulm attended local public schools, considering himself a very ordinary child, though 'quick of temper, inclined to obstinacy, truthful but outrageously inquisitive'. A tinkerer from a young age, he constantly dismantled his toys to discover their inner workings. As a teenager, this developed into an interest in business and led him to take a job as a stockbroker's clerk. Ulm would later claim that he had ambitions for a career in either the share market or legal profession.

Accounts of Kingsford Smith's childhood emphasise his outgoing, almost hyperactive personality and wild 'streak'. In his home suburb of Neutral Bay and at St Andrew's Cathedral School he had the reputation of a larrikin and

Ulm's parents insisted on his discharge as a minor following his wounding at Gallipoli in 1915. He re-enlisted with their blessing two years later once he had turned 18.

a risk-taker. Kingsford Smith's surviving school reports suggest intelligence and capability tempered by an unwillingness to conform and perhaps a difficulty to concentrate on any one thing for an extended amount of time. By all accounts, he was a popular and charismatic teenager, perpetually the centre of attention, and a keen smoker and drinker from his mid-adolescent years. Like Ulm, mechanical things intrigued Kingsford Smith from a young age and as a teenager he bought a motorcycle. He left school at 16 to work as a machinist for the Colonial Sugar Refining Company.

The Great War dramatically changed the lives of these two young men. In September 1914, just six weeks after the declaration of war, the 16-year-old Ulm lied about his age and enlisted under a pseudonym. Landing at Gallipoli on 25 April 1915, within the campaign's first few days he was buried alive by an exploding shell and wounded. While recovering in Egypt, Ulm contracted venereal disease and was sent home, where his parents insisted on his discharge as a minor.

With their permission, Ulm re-enlisted in 1917, following his 18th birthday. He arrived in France in late June 1918 but suffered shrapnel

Kingsford Smith (left) relished the opportunity to work as a motorcycle dispatch rider in Egypt and France.

'Private Charles Jackson'—the pseudonym Ulm used to enlist in 1914—has a formal portrait taken in Egypt in 1915.

Kingsford Smith wore these Royal Flying Corps wings in combat over the Western Front in 1917. Eighty-eight years later, Australian astronaut Andy Thomas would carry them into space aboard the Space Shuttle Discovery.

Like most Australian soldiers, Ulm played the part of tourist well and made the most of the exotic locations in which he found himself.

Gallipoli experience and a resolute personality marked Ulm as an ideal non-commissioned officer when he re-enlisted in 1917.

In early 1917 Kingsford Smith (right) attended the School of Military Aeronautics at Oxford to learn the business of being an officer in the Royal Flying Corps.

wounds to his right leg just two weeks later. The injury's severity kept him out of front-line service for the rest of the war. It was during this brief second stint of active service that Ulm had an introduction to aviation when, while training in Britain, a friend in the Royal Flying Corps took him on several joy-flights. Ulm considered the experience a 'revelation' and immediately perceived the 'vast potentialities' of 'money and public prominence' aeroplanes represented.

Also keen to get to the front, Kingsford Smith enlisted on 10 February 1915, the day after his 18th birthday. In hindsight, he would consider it the defining moment of his life. He fought at Gallipoli in late 1915 and afterwards served in Egypt as a motorcycle dispatch rider.

Along with most of the Australian Imperial Force, Kingsford Smith went to France in early 1916. Although enamoured with his motorcycle, he seized an opportunity to apply for the Royal Flying Corps, his youth, private school education and experience with machines making him an ideal candidate for training as a pilot. With 36 hours of solo flying experience, he went to the front as a fighter pilot in June 1917, just in time to participate in some of the heaviest aerial fighting of the war above the Ypres Salient. A seemingly natural flier, Kingsford Smith earned a Military

Cross for shooting down four enemy aircraft in his first month at the front. Shot down himself in August, he suffered wounds and mental strain that would detain him in Britain as an instructor for the rest of the war. The experience, however, failed to dampen his enthusiasm. He finished the war determined to make a career of aviation. As he told his mother in a letter from Britain, 'flying has a good future, just you wait and see'.

The war had introduced both men to the wonders, thrills and commercial possibilities of flying, an effect it also had on the wider world. For all the turmoil and devastation it left in its wake, the Great War also focused an immense amount of creative energy into the development of aviation. By the end of the war, aircraft could fly substantially higher, faster and longer than they had just four years previously. And from the war emerged vast stockpiles of surplus aircraft and thousands of unemployed pilots—men, who, like Kingsford Smith, hoped to make a living out of their newfound thrill. Within months of the Armistice these ex-war fliers were establishing the world's first airmail and passenger services around Europe and the United States, rapidly transforming transportation as people knew it.

Recognising the potential of aviation for a vast, sparsely populated country like Australia, in March 1919 the federal government announced a £10,000 prize for the first aviator to fly

'A care-free, cigarette-smoking, leave-seeking lot of young devils who feared nothing, except being brought down behind enemy lines', is how Kingsford Smith (second row, second from the right) later recalled his fellow officers in No. 19 Squadron RFC. The reality of aerial combat was in fact somewhat darker.

from England to Australia in under 30 days.
Kingsford Smith and some ex-Flying Corps
mates attempted to enter but struggled to
find an aircraft manufacturer to back them. In
the slack months following the war they had
skylarked around England in a barnstorming
outfit, becoming notorious for reckless flying
and, some alleged, insurance fraud.

Bitterly disappointed, Kingsford Smith went
to the United States hoping to find backing
for a trans-Pacific flight to Australia. Given the
aircraft of the day, it was a hopelessly optimistic
proposition that found no support. He ended
up working in Hollywood as a stunt pilot before
returning to Australia in early 1921, restless and
broke. For a few months Kingsford Smith flew
for a cooperative known as Diggers Aviation
Co., ferrying people around New South Wales.
Dangerous flying and drinking cost him his job
following a series of accidents. For the next two
years Kingsford Smith worked on Australia's
first scheduled airmail service, flying between
Geraldton and Derby for West Australian
Airways Ltd, a company started by fellow ex-
Royal Flying Corps pilot Norman Brearley.

Following a short-lived marriage and 'bored with
the monotony of it all', Kingsford Smith revived
his trans-Pacific aspirations and teamed up
with colleague Keith Anderson. Like Kingsford
Smith, Anderson had flown during the war,
been wounded and was in his mid-20s. Both
men had also spent time overseas during their
childhoods, Kingsford Smith in Canada and
Anderson in South Africa. The similarities ended

'I very soon realised that my flying life would be short indeed if I continued at that game for very long': Kingsford Smith working as a stunt man in Hollywood in 1920, dangling from the undercarriage.

there, however. In contrast to Kingsford Smith's electrifying charisma and impetuosity, Anderson was quiet and reserved, almost painfully pleasant and measured in his thoughts and actions. Ulm would later sum him up as 'a simple soul with a broad grin and an intensely parochial outlook'. Keith Anderson was, in short, the sort of man easily trammelled by more assertive peers.

To raise capital for their attempt on the Pacific, Kingsford Smith, Anderson and Bob Hitchcock, a mechanic they had worked with in Western Australia, established an airline to operate out of Sydney. They returned east in January 1927, flying a pair of Bristol Tourer biplanes. Although they failed to break any records, the newspapers covered the flight, introducing the public to Kingsford Smith for the first time.

Meanwhile, Ulm had returned to Sydney from the war also determined to go into the aviation business. 'Make no mistake', he confidently told an ex-soldier mate, 'the whole world will be on wings soon and I'm going to put it there'. With £1,000 he had shrewdly made from a £50 investment in London, Ulm established the Aviation Service Company to provide regular services around New South Wales. The venture, in his words, turned out a 'complete and unmitigated disaster', promptly going into insolvency. It marked the beginning of a string of failures for Ulm, the Australian Aero Club recording that by 1926 he held 'the record' of being associated with 'no fewer than five extinct aviation companies'. 'I began to realise', he later wrote, 'that the greatest risk to life in aviation was probably starvation'. Ulm had married in

Keith Anderson (left) and Bob Hitchcock (right) had a troubled association with Kingsford Smith and Ulm that would eventually have tragic consequences.

1919—a son, John, following two years later—but his financial woes led to divorce. Following the break-up, John stayed with his mother and would only see his father occasionally.

Ulm was surveying his business prospects in January 1927 when he read about Kingsford Smith and Anderson's flight from Perth. Approaching the two pilots, he convinced them to take him into the partnership to manage a bid for a government contract to run an air service between Adelaide and Perth. Plans were progressing when in May 1927, Charles Lindbergh flew across the Atlantic earning worldwide fame and immense fortune. It prompted the three men to discuss an equivalent venture, Ulm and Kingsford Smith being surprised to learn that each other had envisaged a Pacific flight, independently, for

several years. 'Ulm had similar ideas to mine', recalled Kingsford Smith. 'He was ambitious; he wanted to do something which would make the world sit up; he had a good business head; in fact, he was a born organiser.'

Indeed, in less than a month, Ulm hatched a plan to fly around Australia to generate publicity and gain experience for their attempt on the Pacific. He financed the flight by selling exclusive coverage to *The Sun*, and in doing so cultivated an important relationship with the newspaper's wealthy and influential owner, H. Campbell Jones. Ulm also arranged a sponsorship deal with the Vacuum Oil Company to supply fuel to remote locations around the continent, in some instances, using camels. Although remarkably effective, Ulm's autocratic management style and abrasive

Surplus warplanes such as this Avro 504 spent the early 1920s—like Kingsford Smith, second from the right—barnstorming and stunting for a public enamoured with the novelty of flight.

efficiency alienated some of Kingsford Smith's associates. Keith Anderson, in particular, was furious to learn that he would be excluded from the venture, with Ulm (who did not have a pilot's licence) accompanying Kingsford Smith in the twin-seat Bristol biplane. Unlike Anderson, a pilot of considerable experience, Ulm had been prevented by his war injury from gaining any formal flying qualifications. At this stage he probably only had a handful of hours in the air with friends and colleagues.

Ulm and Kingsford Smith set out from Sydney on 19 June 1927. What followed, in Kingsford Smith's words, was '10 days of the hardest work I had ever experienced'. Each day they flew long stretches, up to 1,400 kilometres over wild country and between improvised airfields with absolutely no aviation infrastructure. Most nights they spent repairing the battered old biplane and at one stage went 39 hours without sleep. At each stop, Ulm cabled updates to *The Sun*, whose stories and editorials began to cultivate public interest in the pair. The toughest stage occurred between Broome and Perth when storms forced them to fly at 50 feet. The conditions 'would have made any flying man blanch', reckoned Ulm. As things would turn out, it was all highly pertinent to what lay in store over the Pacific.

Ulm and Kingsford Smith made it back to Sydney having circumnavigated the continent by air in just over ten days. They had broken the previous record in half. 'Australia began to talk about us', remembered Kingsford Smith. 'At

a bound, we had jumped into prominence.' At a luncheon in Sydney hosted by *The Sun*, Ulm seized on the attention and announced plans to fly across the Pacific. New South Wales Premier Jack Lang responded with a pledge of £3,500, the equivalent of almost a quarter of a million dollars today, and Vacuum Oil agreed to find an aeroplane for them in the United States.

Although his relationship with Ulm had become strained, Anderson agreed to stay with the partnership. A fortnight of frenzied planning followed, during which Ulm somehow found time to remarry. On 14 July 1927, the trio signed a contract with Campbell Jones to again provide *The Sun* with exclusive updates during the flight. In exchange the newspaper paid them £1,000 and funded a first-class sea passage. With the ink on the contract drying, they ran from *The Sun*'s offices down George Street to Circular Quay and boarded the SS *Tahiti*, bound for San Francisco.

Describing Ulm and Kingsford Smith's preparations 'complete', the newspapers predicted the three aviators' return flight to Australia in a matter of weeks. As things happened, their triumphal landing in Brisbane would not take place for almost 11 months, during which time their supposedly 'complete' preparations would unravel completely, almost forcing Ulm to add another to his failed aviation ventures. Most unexpected of all, however, was that when they did return it would not be Anderson stepping out of *Southern Cross*, but rather, two Americans.

Premier Jack Lang welcomes Kingsford Smith and Ulm back to Sydney at the conclusion of their round-Australia flight, Mascot aerodrome, June 1927.

'OVER GOLDEN GATE
1100 FEET'

Take-off in San Francisco, 31 May 1928

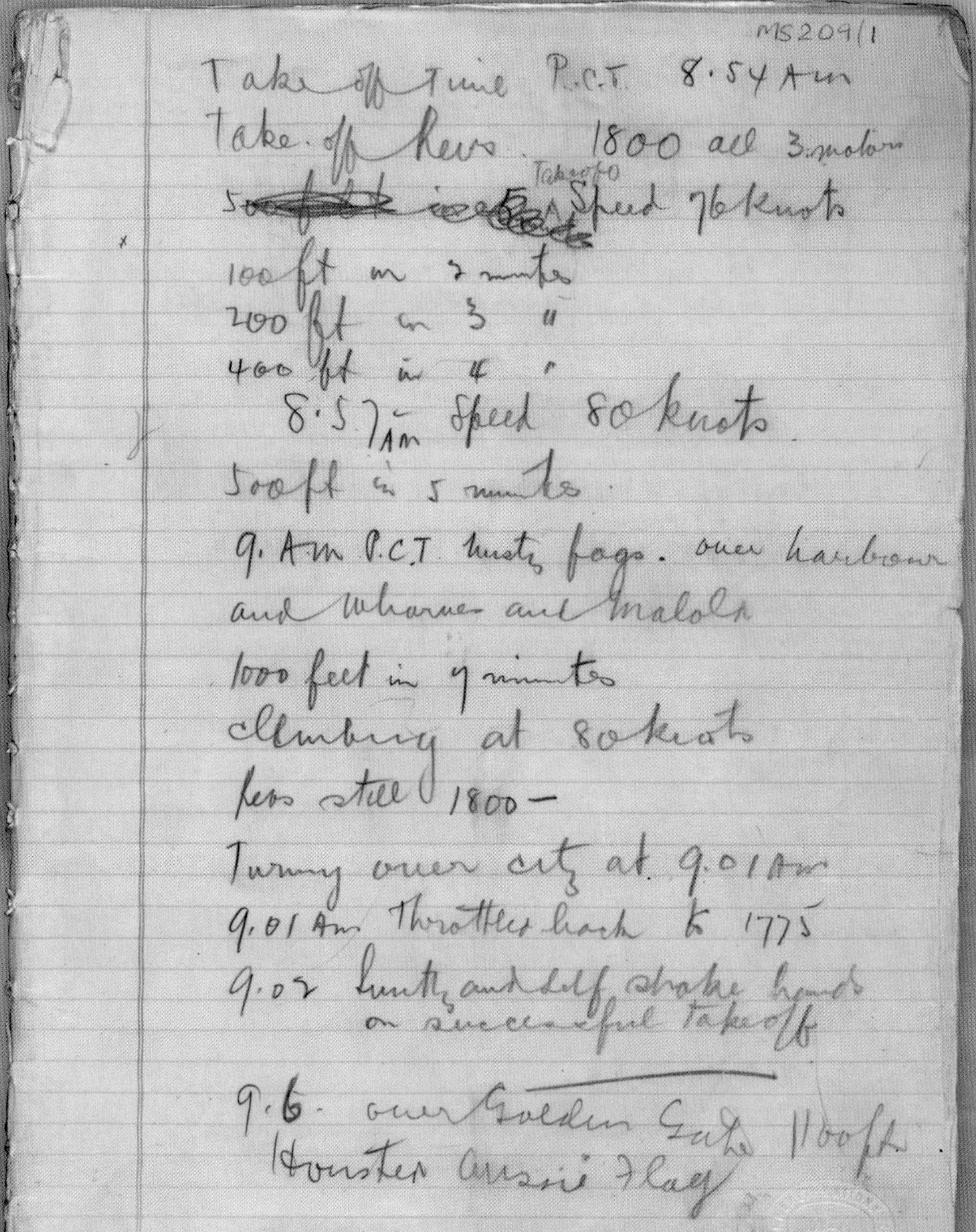

Take off time P.C.T. 8.54 A.m

Take off revs. 1800 all 3 motors

~~Takeoff~~ Speed 76 knots

100 ft in 2 minutes

200 ft in 3 "

400 ft in 4 '

8.57 A.m Speed 80 knots.

500 ft in 5 minutes.

9. A.m P.C.T. husty fogs. over harbour

and wharves and Malola

1000 feet in 9 minutes

climbing at 80 knots

revs still 1800 —

Turning over city at 9.01 A.m

9.01 A.m Throttled back to 1775

9.02 hustz and self shake hands
     on successful takeoff

9.6. over Golden Gate 1100 ft.

Hoisted Aussie Flag

Take off Time P.C.T. 8.54AM

Take off Revs 1800 all 3 motors

~~500 feet and~~ Take off speed 76 knots

100 ft in 2 minutes

200 ft in 3 "

400 ft in 4 "

8.57AM Speed 80 knots

500 ft in 5 minutes

9AM P.C.T. misty fogs over harbour and wharves and Malola

1000 feet in 7 minutes

Climbing at 80 knots

Revs still 1800—

Turning over city at 9.01AM

9.01AM Throttled back to 1775

9.02 Smithy and self shake hands on successful take off

9.6 over Golden Gate 1100 ft

Hoisted Aussie flag

The altitude control on centre motor jammed forward and cut out center motor after running about 800 feet.

Stopped all motors and restarted.

We estimate takeoff distance at 2500 feet. Runway.

The altitude control on centre motor jammed forward and cut out centre motor after running about 800 feet.

Stopped all motors and restarted.

We estimate take off distance at 2500 feet.
Runway.

Like many airmen from their era, Kingsford Smith and Ulm respected superstition. The 'Felix' pin Kingsford Smith wore on his flying cap is evident in this 1929 photograph.

Dawn barely broke over San Francisco Bay on 31 May 1928. Fog blanketed the water, obscuring the city's prominent skyline to the hundreds of people gathered at Oakland aerodrome around a blue tri-engine monoplane, emblazoned with the words *Southern Cross* in large white letters along its fuselage. In spite of the morning's damp heaviness, the atmosphere hummed with anticipation.

Under the aircraft's vast wing, Charles Kingsford Smith, Charles Ulm and their American companions, Harry Lyon and Jim Warner, milled about with mechanics, friends and reporters while police held back the spectators. For pioneering aviators, they all looked rather ordinary; their ties and suits suggested a day in the office more than a flight across the world's largest ocean. Kingsford Smith and Ulm's flying helmets and riding boots were all that suggested their true vocation, and distinguished them from their American colleagues, who had barely done any flying before. On his flying cap, Kingsford Smith wore his good-luck charm, a Felix the Cat badge. When a journalist asked him where he got it he blushed before responding, 'A young lady. It was so romantic'. At the journalist's request, Ulm and Lyon spoke about their charms too. Lyon, a natural extrovert, munched on peanuts as he showed off the 'plain pin' he wore 'for luck', while Ulm revealed a small Buddha statue containing a rattlesnake's tail. He wasn't sure of the significance: one of his old digger mates had

Friends farewell the crew of Southern Cross *at Oakland in May 1928.*

sent it out from Sydney. The quietest of the group, radio operator Jim Warner, said he didn't have any tokens. 'I have had a lot of bad luck in my life', he explained. 'Now I am due for a bit of good luck.'

While Ulm bustled about overseeing final preparations, Kingsford Smith regaled the reporters with his poise and charm. 'I've waited many weary months for this day', he told them. 'We are fully prepared and if we fail, I haven't a single regret.' He then added: 'We absolutely won't fail. I shall be in Sydney before 10 June'. People gathered around him shaking his hand, pressing kisses on his grinning face and slapping him on the back. Things took an awkward turn, taking the sheen off Kingsford Smith's optimism, when a sobbing old woman stepped forward and embraced him, pressing a ring into his hand. It belonged to her son Alvin Eichwaldt, one of six pilots killed attempting to fly to Hawaii in the disastrous Dole Air Race ten months before. Visibly embarrassed, Kingsford Smith agreed to wear it and promptly climbed up into the cockpit. He regained his composure enough to manage a 'cheerio' to the crowd as he did. The Americans boarded through the fuselage door and, finally satisfied everything was in order, Ulm took his place in the cockpit next to Kingsford Smith.

With a cough and a belch of smoke the three engines thundered to life, instantly overwhelming all other noise and making conversation inside the aircraft impossible. As the engines warmed, Ulm opened the brown notebook he had purchased to serve as a log and started a brief conversation with Kingsford Smith with pencilled notes. How much runway would they need? Although *Southern Cross* could lift off in 120 metres with a regular fuel load, the additional 2 tonnes of equipment and petrol on board would considerably extend its take-off run. Kingsford Smith scribbled a couple of predictions, settling on '2500 feet' (760 metres). They had 1500 metres of runway in any case, with a United States Army Air Corps fire wagon at the end should there be an accident.

A crowd farewells Southern Cross *at Long Beach, Los Angeles, on 23 May 1928—a week before it embarked on the flight to Hawaii.*

Pushing the three throttle levers, Kingsford Smith coaxed *Southern Cross* forward. It began to gather speed but had run for less than 250 metres when, in a moment of monumental anti-climax, the centre engine stalled. Mechanics rushed out to push the aircraft back, but Kingsford Smith waved them away: climbing aboard, he and Ulm had noticed the San Francisco sheriff trying to battle his way through the crowd. They suspected he had a legal order grounding them for debts they had no hope of paying. Kingsford Smith had only a single American dollar on him, while nine copper cents jingled about in the pockets of Ulm's suit.

Kingsford Smith opened the throttles up. 'The roar of those three great engines quickly assumed for us the pleasing grandeur of a symphony of great music', recalled Ulm. With the emergency vehicle approaching, *Southern Cross* rose, and then settled back down. It hit 140 kilometres per hour and lifted again to narrowly clear the embankment at the runway's end.

Observers on the ground saw the silver wing gleam in the morning sun as the lumbering aircraft cleared the fog and climbed out over the city. It took Kingsford Smith two minutes to cajole the overladen machine to 100 feet. As they passed the city, the tallest skyscrapers towering above them, thousands of people stopped and peered up. Over the past few months, the monoplane had regularly thundered over their homes and offices on test flights. Kingsford Smith eased the throttles back, the engine roar subsiding ever so slightly.

He and Ulm shook hands enthusiastically and four minutes later they passed over the Golden Gate, the opening of San Francisco Bay into the Pacific Ocean. Ulm fixed a small Australian flag to the instrument panel, but within minutes the wind roaring through the cockpit's open sides had shredded it.

As *Southern Cross* headed out towards the open ocean, Kingsford Smith felt a wave of relief—a reprieve from the 'worries and anxieties' of the past nine months—and in the same instant, 'a tremendous elation' at the prospect ahead.

Organising the flight

The jubilant handshake Ulm and Kingsford Smith shared over San Francisco marked not only a successful take-off but also the end of a ten-month struggle to get the Pacific flight 'off the ground', in the figurative sense. Those months tested the two aviators' resilience almost as much, they reckoned, as the flight itself.

Kingsford Smith, Ulm and Keith Anderson left Sydney in July 1927 with what they thought were definite plans. With an aircraft purchased by their sponsor Vacuum Oil, they would enter the Dole Air Race, and compete for its $25,000 prize for the fastest flight from San Francisco to Hawaii. In Honolulu they would fit the aircraft with floats and continue to Australia in several short hops. The whole thing, they told the newspapers, would cost £7,000. As Ulm later admitted, though, he had devised the whole plan with 'gay abandon' and 'wild groping in the dark'.

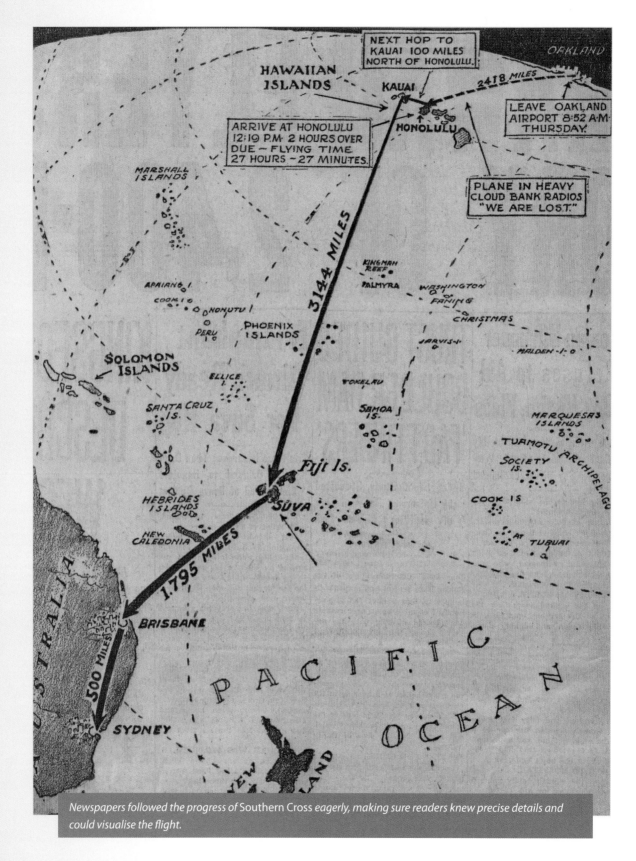

Newspapers followed the progress of Southern Cross eagerly, making sure readers knew precise details and could visualise the flight.

Arrival in San Francisco cured their naivety. The best Vacuum Oil had been able to arrange at short notice was an old biplane, obviously unsuited to a long ocean flight. This forced the Australians to forego an entry into the air race, which started a week after their arrival in the United States. It was disappointing, but serendipitous as things turned out. The race was a fiasco; three pilots were killed on practice flights and another six died during the race and subsequent search effort. Of the eight starting aircraft, only two made it to Hawaii. Flying across the Pacific—even as far as Hawaii—evidently involved much more than the three Australians had initially anticipated. Cables from Australia urged the trio to abandon their attempt and *The Sun* offered to pay for their sea passage home.

Kingsford Smith, Ulm and Anderson established an office at Vacuum Oil and, with help from company representative Locke Harper, they set about reconceiving the whole venture. Research into previous long flights suggested the importance of multiple engines and radio-assisted navigation equipment. They noted the good reputation of the tri-motor Fokker F.VII which, in fact, had made the first California to Hawaii crossing the previous year.

Although Fokker F.VIIs were rare in the United States at this time, the Australians had the remarkable good fortune to hear that one had gone on the market just days after their arrival. It belonged to the renowned Australian

San Leandro, California, a suburb of Oakland, in 1928.

The Mission District, heart of old San Francisco, as it appeared to Anderson, Ulm and Kingsford Smith in January 1928.

explorer George Hubert Wilkins who had used it during an abortive Arctic expedition in 1926. Ulm inspected the Fokker in Seattle and, finding it 'in excellent condition', convinced Wilkins to sell it for £3,000 without engines or instruments. It was an attractive deal, but buying the plane practically exhausted the partnership's funds. Kingsford Smith used his contacts in the politically influential Returned Sailors' and Soldiers' Imperial League of Australia to secure the promise of another £1,000 from Premier Lang, and Ulm convinced

the Melbourne department store owner Sidney Myer to pitch in £1,500. Myer agreed on the condition that he would have no further association with the flight; he believed they were certain to be killed.

With the extra finances 'the clouds seemed to be revealing a silver lining both literally and figuratively', as Ulm put it. He pulled diplomatic strings to have an order for three Wright Whirlwind engines supplied with priority and arranged for the Boeing factory in Seattle to fit the Fokker with special long-range fuel tanks and reinforced landing gear. To instruct Kingsford Smith in handling the tri-motor and flying in low visibility using instruments only, Ulm hired

experienced naval pilot Lieutenant George Pond. Keith Anderson, meanwhile, sailed to Hawaii to scout for suitable landing grounds. 'When you've got a big job to do', explained Ulm of his management philosophy, 'look after the little things and see to it that every human element of the enterprise is up to standard'.

On 11 October 1927—remarkably, just nine weeks after arriving in the United States— Kingsford Smith flew the Fokker from Seattle to San Francisco, covering the 1,100 kilometres in eight hours. 'The plane rode a heavy gale splendidly', he afterwards told reporters. On Anderson's suggestion, they dubbed the aircraft *Southern Cross*.

Ulm told reporters that they planned to start the flight at the end of October. But they still needed radio and navigational equipment and had by this stage accrued a staggering debt. What appeared to Ulm as the 'eternal problem of finances' came to a head in the middle of the month when the Lang government lost office to Thomas Bavin's National Party. The new Premier withdrew the state's financial support and publically urged the airmen to sell the aircraft and return to Australia immediately. By this stage, Ulm claimed they had spent about £20,000 on the aircraft and still needed at least another £6,000—almost as much as he had originally anticipated the whole venture would cost. Despite this, they refused to abandon their plans; as a temporary solution Ulm borrowed the money from Harper and mortgaged *Southern Cross* to cover the most immediate debts. At Ulm's insistence, Anderson

The close association Vacuum Oil Company had with the venture is illustrated in this clock it presented Kingsford Smith after the Pacific flight.

also reluctantly borrowed money from his family to help finance *Southern Cross'* outfitting.

To cover additional costs, Ulm secured sponsorship from a Californian oil company to attempt a flying endurance record. During the American winter, Kingsford Smith and Pond made five attempts to stay airborne over San Francisco Bay for longer than the current record of 52 hours and 22 minutes. By the fourth attempt they had come within two hours of their goal. Kingsford Smith described their fifth and final effort on 17 January 1928:

> *The fifty hours which I spent in the air with Pond circling round and round San Francisco Bay will always remain a nightmare to me. It was bitterly cold; we could only communicate with penciled notes to each other; we were cramped in the cockpit, since the passage way to the rear compartment was filled with petrol tanks; we couldn't smoke we couldn't sleep; we had to maintain our wits at their sharpest, for at our low flying speed we were always near to stalling.*

Although useful experience for the Pacific flight, *Southern Cross* ran out of fuel two and a half hours short of the record. 'We were all three bitterly disappointed', recalled Kingsford Smith.

By the end of January 1928 the whole venture appeared to be disintegrating. 'We were so poor', admitted Kingsford Smith, 'that we had not even loose cash in our pockets to purchase cigarettes or a meal'. Ulm recalled how they took to sneaking out of hotels without paying

'When you've got a big job to do look after the little things':
Ulm gets his hands dirty with the details at a fuel pump in 1928.

and deliberately avoiding their creditors, who were making increasingly strident demands for remuneration. 'Bitter arguments and petty squabbles' became common among the three Australians and Anderson and Kingsford Smith began to consider going home.

Ulm, however, remained dogmatically committed to the venture. During February and March he exerted a staggering amount of energy preparing business proposals and presenting them in boardrooms all around California to raise sponsorship for the flight. The detail and scope of business vision in these proposals is truly remarkable, yet they also suggest desperation. To the Atlantic Union Oil Company, for example, he offered ownership of *Southern Cross*, to work for them as an ambassador in Australia without pay and to reimburse any costs incurred on the flight within six months. Kingsford Smith contributed in his own way, telling reporters that he would sell seats on *Southern Cross* to young ladies for £3,000 each. Neither approach found any backers, forcing them to put the aircraft up for sale. Anderson decided to go home at the end of February.

In mid-March, in the midst of 'frantic' attempts to sell the aircraft, they approached the Californian Bank's president to help find a buyer. He introduced them to George Allan Hancock, a millionaire oil magnate with a strong interest in maritime navigation. To their initial disappointment, Hancock declined to make an offer on *Southern Cross* but surprisingly invited them on a yacht cruise to Mexico. Ulm, who thought the American must have felt sorry for them, accepted, reasoning that 'at least we would be well fed for a while'.

During the 12-day voyage Hancock treated the two Australians to lavish hospitality. It was a glorious change from the flophouses and sparse meals on which they had subsisted for months. Ulm relished the break from business stress and even began to reconcile himself to the failure of their plans. Hancock showed 'a sincere and almost intense interest', in Ulm's words, in their Pacific flight plans and at the end of the voyage quite suddenly offered to purchase *Southern Cross*. He would take care of their debts and then allow them to fly the plane to Australia as planned. He was also prepared to advance them cash to cover living expenses and purchase the remaining equipment for the flight. It was a timely offer; leaving the yacht on 2 April 1928, Ulm learned that bailiffs had seized *Southern Cross*.

Kingsford Smith and Ulm cabled the good news to Anderson, but he refused to return to the United States. Kingsford Smith's biographer, Ian Mackersey, provides a sharp analysis of the cables that flew back and forth across the Pacific for several days following Hancock's purchase of *Southern Cross*, pointing out culpability on both sides. Kingsford Smith and Ulm were vague in reporting the fortunate turn of events, leaving Anderson unclear on the sort of aircraft they had 're-purchased', who had refinanced them and their planned route. For his part, Anderson was broke and could not raise funds for a first-class sea passage, but refused to settle for a second-class ticket

or work his way across the Pacific. Why Kingsford Smith and Ulm did not approach Hancock to fund Anderson's passage is unclear: perhaps they resented him for 'abandoning' the partnership; perhaps Ulm—still not a licensed pilot—felt that Anderson's involvement would make his part in the flight redundant. In any case, Ulm concluded the matter by bluntly informing Anderson that he forfeited any claim to future profits from the flight.

Since arriving in San Francisco Ulm had been looking for a navigator. He hoped to secure an 'Aussie', or at least 'a Britisher', and had approached Wilkins, but the famous explorer had his own adventures planned. Time constraints forced them to settle for an American. While having *Southern Cross*' navigational equipment calibrated by the United States Navy Hydrographic Office, they met Harry Lyon, an ex-merchant marine navigator with a colourful past and considerable ocean-going experience. He had rounded Cape Horn on a sailing ship as a 21-year-old in 1906 and spent the next decade working cargo ships around the Pacific. His memoir reads like a pulp adventure novella, describing a life of hard drinking, fist fights, shipwrecks and mutinies. After a more respectable stint commanding a United States Navy transport during the Great War, he returned to a chequered existence, smuggling alcohol and becoming caught up in the Mexican Revolution. Finding his 'adventurous nature and clear thinking' immediately appealing, Kingsford Smith and Ulm asked him to be their navigator.

'A good business head': organising the Pacific flight would stretch Ulm's managerial skills and resolve to the limit.

With the aircraft now equipped with state-of-the-art radio and navigational equipment, the crew spent the second half of May making test flights 80 kilometres out to sea. The exercises were useful to Lyon, who had only flown once before and had never navigated from the air. On the ground, *Southern Cross* underwent final modifications and fine-tuning. With Hancock's chequebook at his disposal, Ulm spared no expense. To service the aircraft's three Wright Whirlwind engines he hired the best engineer he could find, Cecil 'Doc' Maidment, who worked for the Wright Company and had gained prominence in the aviation community as Lindbergh's mechanic.

They still lacked a radio operator; Kingsford Smith and Ulm had considered several but failed to settle on one. Then, five days before their planned departure date, Lyon suggested an old shipmate, Jim Warner. The product of a tough, orphaned upbringing, Warner had joined the Navy in 1911 and during the Great War served as a wireless operator on the USS *St Louis* where he met Lyon. Warner left the Navy in 1927 and again fell on hard times. When Kingsford Smith and Ulm met him he was selling suits door to door. Despite having never flown before and being prone to anxiety, Warner promptly accepted their offer and spent the few remaining days familiarising himself with *Southern Cross'* radio.

Warner and Ulm clashed almost immediately. On the night before leaving, Ulm presented ('sprung' in Warner's words) the Americans with contracts dated ten days previously. 'After reading it I didn't know whether to laugh or get peeved', recalled Warner. It offered them a weekly wage until they arrived in Fiji in addition to $1,000 at the completion of the flight. They would return to the United States by sea while Ulm and Kingsford Smith completed the flight to Brisbane. In return, Warner and Lyon had to waive all claims for injury and agree not to speak to the press before their return to America.

Warner felt he didn't have any choice. 'If I didn't sign it I couldn't go', he reasoned. 'If I didn't go it would have looked as though I had suddenly developed an eleventh-hour case of cold feet.' Lyon's feelings went unrecorded, but like Warner, he signed the contract. The episode represented the best and worst of Charles Ulm, and, indeed, encapsulates the conundrum that he presents historians. On the one hand, in purely objective business terms, the contract represents a sound decision intended to protect his and Kingsford Smith's considerable investment in the flight and the future commercial endeavours they hoped it might lead to. Also, it was generous: for Warner, the equivalent of about A$34,000 for a fortnight's work by today's standards. On the other hand, though, the contract could be construed as impersonal and somewhat ungracious, especially considering the benevolence Hancock had extended to Ulm and Kingsford Smith. And what's more, the journey would expose all four crew to considerable danger in equal measures. Six aviators had died attempting the first leg less than a year before. Beyond Hawaii, flying lacked precedent altogether.

'The world's greatest aviator': Kingsford Smith became famous for his winning smile as well as for his aerial feats.

'OUR LAST SIGHT OF LAND FOR 24 HOURS'

The first day's flying, 31 May 1928

9.12 am   Wrote first radio message
and just then Lyon passed thro
note to say we were making
beautiful course.

9.12   Revs.   Pt. 1760 Center 1775 St 1760
            Speed 77 knots
            Altitude 1500 ft.
            Oil Pressure:- 60 - 60 - 62
            Oil Temp.   45 · 45 · 40.

9.15   Sighted Farrallones through
            fog and haze.

9.22.   Passing over Farralones, at 1900 ft
            this our last sight of
            land for 24 hours

9.43   Warner reports we are
            North of Radio Beacon
            and Lyon explains per note
            that he set Northerly course
            on account of drift
            We advise Lyon to change
            course and get on T zone of beacon

9.12am Wrote first radio message and just then Lyon passed thru note to say we were making beautiful course

9.12   Revs Pt. 1760 Centre 1775 St 1760

            Speed 77 knots

            Altitude 1500 ft

            Oil Pressure 60 – 60 – 62

            Oil Temp 45 – 45 – 40

9.15   Sighted Farallones through fog and haze

9.22   Passing over Faralones at 1900 ft

            This our last sight of land for 24 hours

9.43   Warner reports we are North of Radio Beacon and
            Lyon explains per note that he set northerly course on
            account of drift. We advise Lyon to change course and
            get on T zone of beacon.

9.48am   Altitude 1600 ft.   Speed 76 knots
     Revs. 1685 – 1700 – 1680.
     Oil Temp. 50 – 53 – 45.

9.51. ~~Gradual~~ Warner Reports gradually
working back on T Zone.

9.53 I advise Lyon to keep us on Beacon T
Zone by moving the E.1.C Controller.

9.56. Now dead on T Zone of Beacon
Smith and I both chuckle ~~to each~~
other.

We know, now, that our striving
for complete equipment of every

kind was worth while. Everything
is functioning perfectly

10.Am See Journey Log.

10.5' Clouds - light cumulus at 1600 our
height - now climbing slowly above
them Air speed 72 knots.

10.10 Clouds banking up thickly ahead
look max. height of 2000.
as we pass clouds ~~there~~ it is
bumpy. and getting fairly coolish.

9.48am	Altitude 1600 ft. Speed 76 knots
	Revs 1685 – 1700 – 1680
	Oil Temp 50 – 53 – 45
9.51	Warner reports gradually working back on T zone
9.53	I advise Lyon to keep us on Beacon T Zone by moving the E.I.C controller
9.56	Now dead on T zone of Beacon.
	Smithy and I both chuckle to each other
	We know, now, that our strivings for complete equipment of every kind was worth while. Everything is functioning properly.
10AM	See journey log
10.07	Clouds. Light cumulus at 1600 our height — now climbing slowly above them. Airspeed 72 knots.
10.10	Clouds banking up thickly ahead.
	Look max. height of 2000
	As we pass clouds it is bumpy and getting fairly coolish.

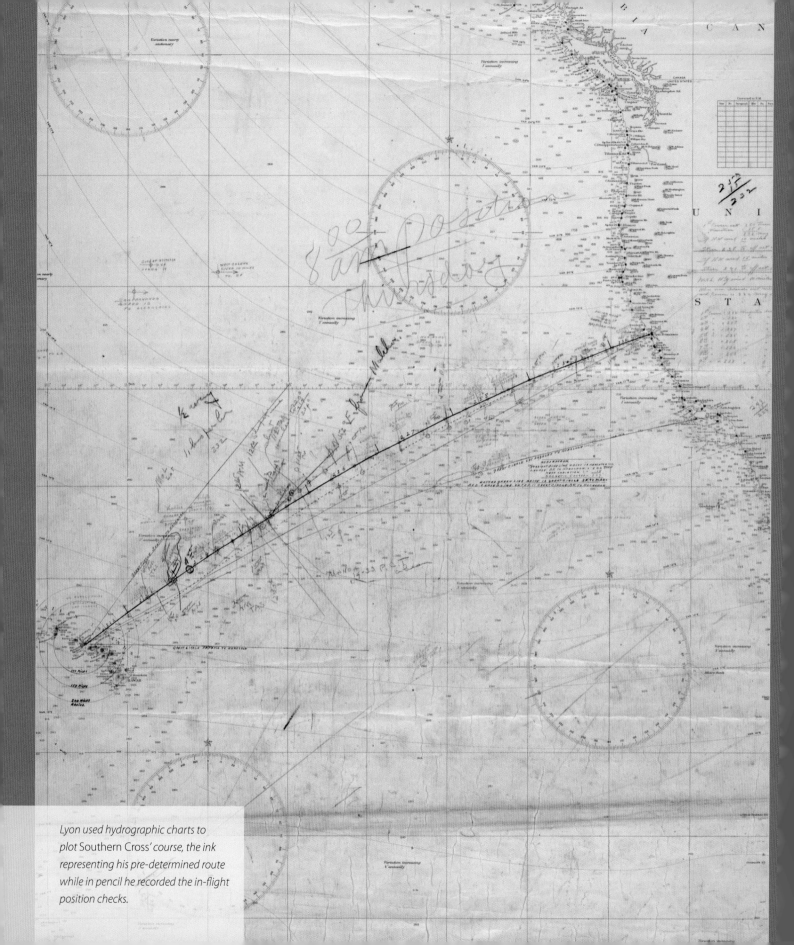

Lyon used hydrographic charts to plot Southern Cross' course, the ink representing his pre-determined route while in pencil he recorded the in-flight position checks.

Twelve minutes after passing over San Francisco, the city's skyline disappeared in the morning haze. 'It seemed to stand, baseless and serene, like a magic city hanging in the clouds', recalled Ulm. A few minutes later the craggy Farallon Islands emerged from the sea mist, 1,900 feet below. They represented, Ulm noted in the log, 'our last sight of land for 24 hours'. In the aircraft's rear cabin, Harry Lyon suddenly felt a sense of 'utter loneliness'. Peering out of the fuselage window at the 4,000 kilometres of ocean and sky before them made him feel 'like a pretty small speck in the universe'.

Only four aircraft before *Southern Cross* had successfully flown from mainland United States to Hawaii. The first had been 11 months previously, when United States Army lieutenants Lester Maitland and Albert Hegenberger did it in a Fokker F.VII tri-motor, the same as *Southern Cross*, in 25 hours 49 minutes. Two civilians, Emory Bronte and Ernest Smith, made the crossing a month later in a single-engine Travel Air 5000, though they crashed on the island of Molokai after running out of fuel. The disastrous Dole Race produced the other two successful crossings in August 1927, when two of the eight starting aircraft made it to Hawaii safely in 26 and 28 hours respectively.

Southern Cross' main tanks (three in the wings and one under the pilot's seat) carried 1,858 litres of fuel. To extend the aircraft's range, Ulm and Kingsford Smith had installed an additional 3,054-litre tank in the cabin from which they could pump fuel into the other

tanks throughout the flight. It was positioned directly behind the wicker chairs they sat on, side by side in the cockpit, and blocked access to the aircraft's rear cabin where Lyon and Warner worked. Everything depended on accurately predicting fuel consumption. Kingsford Smith estimated that with an average speed of 145 kilometres per hour, they had a maximum range of 5,866 kilometres; that is, 832 kilometres more than the journey's longest leg between Hawaii and Fiji.

If the unthinkable should happen, however, Ulm and Kingsford Smith believed themselves well prepared for an emergency. They anticipated that *Southern Cross'* 22-metre-long plywood wing would act as a giant life raft. With an emergency valve, they could quickly jettison fuel before ditching and then cut the engines free with hacksaws. A compartment in the wing carried emergency rations, a water distiller and wireless set. Before leaving, the crew had plotted the route of all ocean liners so they could call for assistance. Kingsford Smith and Ulm invested a lot of trust in these contingencies, refusing to take a life raft so as to save weight. Indeed, they even had *Southern Cross'* wheel brakes removed to lighten the load.

Behind the huge fuel tank, Warner and Lyon occupied the aircraft's rear cabin: essentially a tubular steel frame covered in fabric and held square by a maze of bracing wires. The sides of the aircraft lacked any kind of insulation; just a few millimetres of varnished fabric separated the crew from the thunderous noise of the

For the Pacific flight, Southern Cross used three Wright Whirlwind J5C 220 horsepower engines, each capable of 1,800 revolutions per minute. They had a proven track record, having been employed on several previous long-distance flights, though like all machines of their era, they required diligent maintenance.

engines and the violent slipstream outside. The two Americans sat close together on a pair of wicker chairs purchased from a department store. Neither their seats, nor those in the cockpit, were anchored to the floor and there were no seatbelts.

Lyon sat facing forward, at a desk directly behind the fuel tank. The calculations he made there were critical given that they were aiming for a tiny speck in a wide and empty ocean from thousands of kilometres away with no landmarks to guide them. A slight inaccuracy

early in the journey could put them hundreds of kilometres wide of their destination.

At his disposal, Lyon had a range of navigational tools that spanned the ancient to the state-of-the-art. In addition to three traditional magnetic compasses, *Southern Cross* had an electrically powered Earth Inductor Compass (EIC). A generator on top of the fuselage measured bearings in relation to the earth's magnetic field (which runs north–south). On a set at his desk, Lyon could select a compass bearing for Kingsford Smith and Ulm to follow using a gauge on their instrument panel. Its needle revealed whether they were flying 'dead on' or veering to the left or right of Lyon's chosen course. According to Kingsford Smith the EIC was 'the most valuable steering instrument we carried'.

The radio set operated by Warner represented another sophisticated navigational tool. Rack mounted inside the port cabin and powered off batteries charged by two wind-driven generators on the fuselage, the set could send and receive Morse code transmissions thousands of kilometres. Warner could tune in to United States Army navigational beacons in California and Hawaii, which projected two pairs of beams towards one another, each reaching almost a thousand kilometres out to sea. One beam consisted of an 'A' (dot dash) signal while the other an 'N' (dash dot). Along the centre of the two beams, the signals combined to give a long dash—a 'T'. Hearing this clearly, Warner could be certain that they were heading directly for Hawaii. When he began to hear 'N' or 'A' signals,

Tuning into the 'T': Jim Warner works his radio set enclosed by Southern Cross' *steel skeleton and fabric skin.*

he knew *Southern Cross* to be straying off course. Ships and land-based stations could also use Warner's radio signals to report *Southern Cross'* bearing in relation to their location.

Yet despite this modern equipment, Lyon ultimately relied on the ancient navigational method of dead reckoning. This involved estimating the aircraft's position at regular intervals based on its direction and speed, while compensating for 'drift' caused by the wind. The challenge was that over the ocean there were few indicators to verify where they were at any given point. Aside from the radio, he had to rely on astronomical navigation, using a sextant to calculate *Southern Cross'* position by measuring the distance of celestial objects above the horizon. Sextants represented centuries-old technology, but Lyon had one crudely modified for the air age. Fitted with a spirit bubble, his sextant could be used to estimate the position of the horizon even when it was obscured by cloud. To take shots Lyon needed to open a hatch in the fuselage and lean out into the violent slipstream while attempting to hold the sextant steady. Before the flight, he had practised by taking shots from a car speeding along California's highways at night.

During the first morning's flying, things in the rear cabin quickly settled into a routine. Each hour Lyon would estimate their position on a maritime chart which Warner would then transmit in the hope that, if they did go down, someone might find them. The engine noise through *Southern Cross'* open cockpit sides and canvas fuselage made conversation impossible. To communicate with each other, the crew passed notes scribbled on scrap paper. Warner and Lyon used part of a fishing rod to pass notes over the fuel tank into the cockpit. 'It was a strange experience', thought Ulm, 'for four men to sit in such a confined space and so near to one another, and yet be unable to exchange a word'. Nonetheless, via notes the crew carried on an almost constant dialogue. 'We're as happy as hell cracking "wise cracks" ad lib', reported Ulm in the log.

'The flying conditions were perfect', recalled Kingsford Smith of the first morning, 'but the monotony of the blue sea below us, the blue vault above us, and the overpowering roar of the engines began to oppress us'. At 11 am he took a break, handing control to Ulm. The cockpit was too small to lie down, but Kingsford Smith managed to doze in his chair.

Controlling *Southern Cross* was a physically demanding exercise. The control wheels and foot-operated rudder bar manipulated the aircraft's control surfaces with wires that ran along the exterior of the fuselage. Keeping the Earth Inductor Compass needle on Lyon's course demanded constant weight on the controls: there were no trims or autopilot devices as would assist a pilot during a long-haul flight today. After half an hour, Ulm handed control back to Kingsford Smith, admitting in the log 'experience does count. Smithy flying perfectly. I waver slightly from one side of course to the other'.

'A strange experience…': At no point during the most significant journey of their lives could the members of Southern Cross' crew speak to each other owing to the engine noise. Left to right: Harry Lyon, Charles Ulm, Charles Kingsford Smith and Jim Warner.

Using radio transmissions from Southern Cross, *Sydney newspaper* The Sun *provided Australians with news coverage unlike they had ever experienced before.*

Southern Cross' 3,000-litre fuel tank extended its range considerably but blocked access between cockpit and cabin. The crew used a fishing rod to pass messages to each other.

Shortly after 1 pm—four hours since take-off—Kingsford Smith and Ulm encountered their first 'blind' or 'instrument' flying conditions. 'Clouds just seemed to blow right up', logged Ulm. For the next half hour, *Southern Cross* climbed through a damp, murky haze in an attempt to reach clear skies. Unable to see the horizon, Kingsford Smith had to rely on a pair of spirit levels set into the timber instrument panel before him, indicating the aircraft's rate of climb and bank. At 2,900 feet, as suddenly as it had smothered them, the cloud ended. 'We burst out of this grey wilderness and the steel blue plain of the ocean once more opened up before us.' Kingsford Smith then descended back to 1,200 feet. 'Trying to make better speed down here', explained Ulm in the log.

Changing altitude to avoid cloud formations began to worry Kingsford Smith and Ulm as the afternoon wore on. At 3pm, Lyon calculated they were 843 kilometres from San Francisco and still some 3,000 kilometres from Honolulu. Although this represented only a slightly slower average speed than Kingsford Smith had predicted, the rate at which they were pumping fuel into the main tanks during the afternoon suggested they were burning through it far quicker than anticipated. Behind the pilot and co-pilot four glass tubes provided the approximate fuel level in each of the main tanks, but there was no way to measure fuel remaining in the large auxiliary tank.

Consulting the gauges and their notes on fuel consumption, Ulm and Kingsford Smith made a series of calculations. They checked and re-checked them again; the results were worrying. Although the two airmen disagreed over precisely how much fuel remained, they did agree that given their average ground speed and estimated position, they did not have enough to reach Honolulu. Even Ulm's significantly more optimistic calculations suggested they would run out of fuel some time during the night, perhaps 300 kilometres from land.

Conferring via notes, they decided to run the outer wing tanks until empty. 'It was patent to us', explained Ulm later, 'that when these outboard wing tanks yielded up the last of the gasoline that they held, we would definitely know what petrol was at our disposal'. The note that follows in the log suggests how these dire mathematics focused Ulm's imagination on the prospect of an open ocean ditching in the middle of the night: 'Have not sighted vessel since leaving San Francisco'.

'PERFECTLY GLORIOUS SUNSET'

Flying into the night, 31 May–1 June 1928

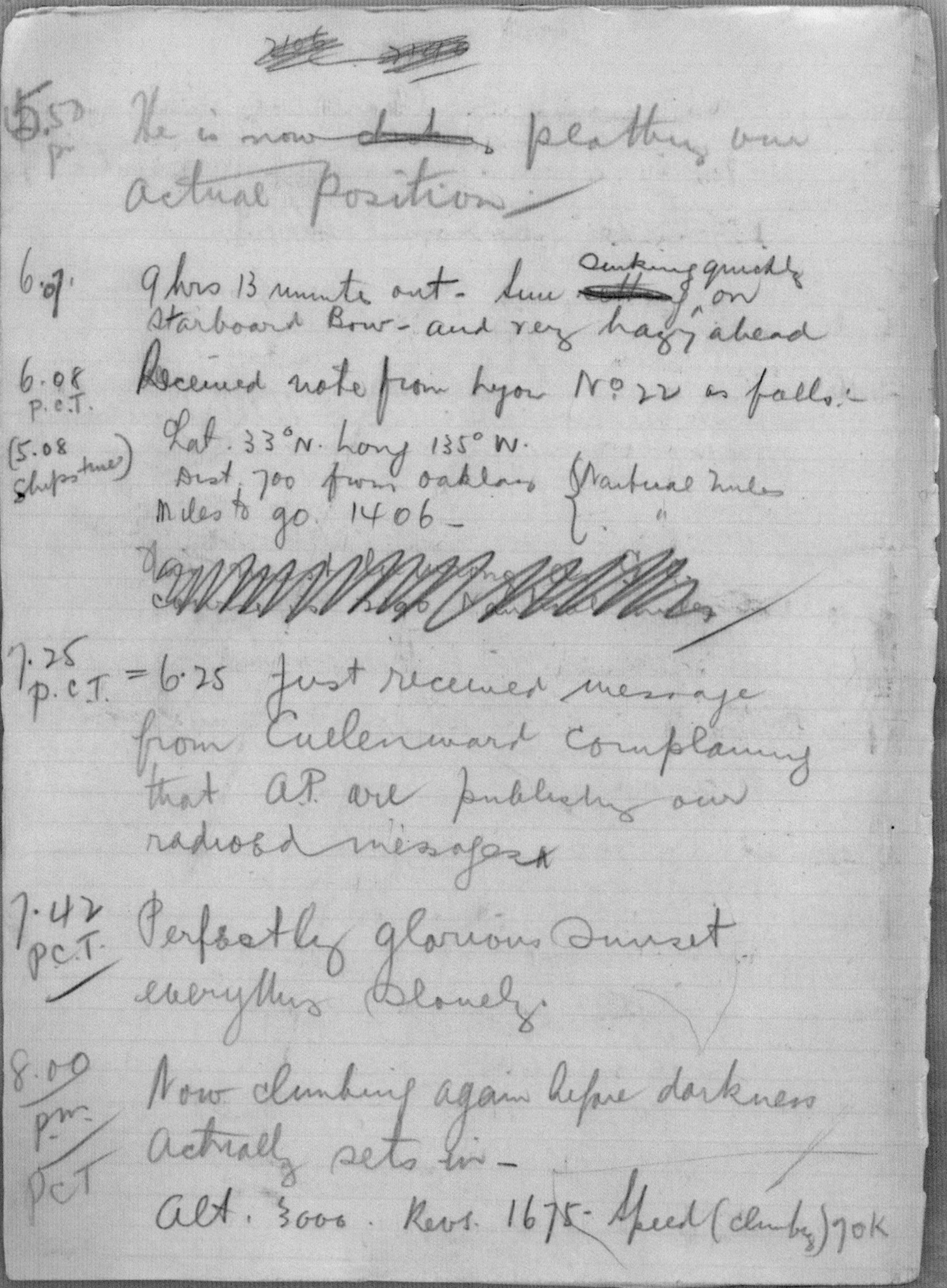

~~Note~~ ~~(crossed out)~~

5.50 p. He is now ~~dodging~~ plotting our actual position.

6.07. 9 hrs 13 minute out - Sun ~~setting quickly~~ on Starboard Bow - and very hazy ahead

6.08 P.C.T. Received note from Lyon Nº 22 as falls:-
(5.08 ships time) Lat. 33° N. Long 135° W. Dist. 700 from Oakland (Nautical miles Miles to go. 1406 - { . "

~~(crossed out lines)~~

7.25 P.C.T. = 6.25 Just received message from Cullenward complaining that A.P. are publishing our radioed messages.

7.42 P.C.T. Perfectly glorious Sunset everything Slovely.

8.00 p.m. PCT Now climbing again before darkness Actually sets in -
Alt. 3000. Revs. 1675 - Speed (climbing) 70K

5.50pm	He is now ~~checking~~ plotting our actual position
6.07	9 hrs 13 minute out. Sun ~~setting~~ sinking quickly on starboard bow—and very hazy ahead
6.08 PCT	Received note from Lyon No. 22 as follows: Lat 33° N Long 135° W
(5.08 ships time)	Dist 700 from Oakland (Nautical miles)

Miles to go 1406   "

~~This must be wrong as GC course is 2190 Nautical Miles~~ |
7.25 PCT	= 6.25 Just received message from Cullenward complaining that AP are publishing our radioed messages.
7.42 PCT	Perfectly glorious sunset everything lovely.
8.00 pm PCT	Now climbing again before darkness actually sets in— Alt 3000 – Revs 1675 – Speed (climbing) 70k

8:00pm. Are approaching a bank of beautiful
snowy white low hanging clouds -
Sun is just about to set. a
perfectly gorgeous view

8:06 Outboard wing tanks cut out

8:16 ½ the Sun is below horizon. we
have been over clouds since
8:05 pm.   Alt. now 4000
              Speed 70 knots.

8:18
PCT   Sunset - The most
beautiful I've seen for
years /

9:19   Left clouds behind -
PCT   alt 3750 feet
              RPM 1625 - 1625 - 1625
          Oil Press 60. 59. 62
          Oil temps 42. 48. out
          Air Sped 70 Knots.
Stars out   moon coming up from behind

8.00pm	Are approaching a bank of beautiful snowy white low hanging clouds—Sun is just about to set. A perfectly glorious view.
8.06	Outboard wing tanks cut out
8.16	½ the sun is below horizon we have been over clouds since 8.05 pm. Alt now 4000
	Speed 70 knots.
8.18 PCT	Sunset—the most beautiful I've seen for years
9.17 PCT	Left clouds behind—
	Alt 3750 feet
	RPM 1625 – 1625 – 1625
	Oil Press 60 59 62
	Oil Temp 42 48 out
	Air speed 70 knots
	Stars out moon coming up from behind

'Perfectly glorious sunset everything lovely': For the journey's first leg, the crew enjoyed almost perfect flying conditions.

Crossing the Pacific would be the first step towards circumnavigating the globe in Southern Cross for Kingsford Smith.

As the afternoon hours dragged by, the endless blue 'vault' above *Southern Cross* began to pale and the clouds took on a golden hue as the sun sank lower in the sky. After nine hours in the air they had covered, according to Lyon's dead reckoning, almost 1,300 kilometres— about a third of the way to Hawaii. 'Away on the starboard bow', recalled Kingsford Smith, 'the sun was setting in a great ball of fire and I witnessed such a spectacular and glorious sunset as I had seldom seen before'.

They had spent most of the day as low as possible (under 2,000 feet) to conserve fuel, but Kingsford Smith decided it safer to fly at a higher altitude during the night where they had a better chance of avoiding bad weather. It represented a difficult decision as climbing would consume more fuel. As *Southern Cross* gradually ascended past towering, golden clouds, their thoughts, in Ulm's words, vacillated between 'black pessimism and a wild exhilaration'. The anxiety subsided at 8.06 pm when, having cleared 3,000 feet, the outboard wing tanks emptied. 'Here was a definite milestone in our gas supply', explained Ulm. Though not guaranteeing that it would last to Hawaii, it was an encouraging sign that they had over-estimated the rate of their fuel consumption earlier. 'We felt ... like reprieved men who had passed through a shadow that had lifted at a most appropriate moment.'

Southern Cross levelled out at 4,000 feet. As the sky darkened, hot exhaust gases from the engines began to glow, at times flaring from 'blue to yellow, and even red'. Warner would later describe how he 'managed to kill quite a bit of time watching the blue flame pouring out each pipe' coming off the engines. 'The fireworks were pretty, but the noise was disgustingly monotonous.' A description of the phenomenon in one of Warner's radio transmissions appeared in newspapers on both sides of the Pacific the following day. The imagery of *Southern Cross* streaking across the night sky towards Australia with a luminous, comet-like tail thrilled readers and provided newspaper editors, who lacked the benefit of photographs, with a compelling illustration.

Although a milestone in aviation history, the trans-Pacific flight also broke new ground in wireless communications. From a retractable, 120-metre wire aerial trailing behind *Southern Cross*, Warner managed to transmit and receive messages over twice as far as anyone had before. By sunset, Warner's Morse code messages were audible to listening stations on both sides of the Pacific, including at Amalgamated Wireless Association's receiving hut at La Perouse in Sydney. Throughout the flight, wireless operators listened for *Southern Cross'* messages 24 hours a day, passing them on to Radio Station 2BL which, via an agreement with *The Sun*, broadcast them into Australian homes. By the end of the flight, 2BL's engineers had rigged up equipment enabling the live broadcast of Warner's dots and dashes directly into listeners' living rooms. It was an unprecedented thing in an age that long-preceded 'live' news coverage, and one in which Australians, so far from Europe and North America, felt isolated from great events.

The Sun and its partners were not, however, the only ones who could hear Warner's transmissions. Anyone with a radio receiver of adequate power could tune in. In fact, the most complete record of *Southern Cross'* radio transmissions during the flight comes from the USS *Omaha*, docked in Pearl Harbor, Honolulu, at the time. A friend of Warner named Charlie Hodge was the ship's wireless operator and throughout the flight he recorded in a log any messages bearing the identifier 'KHAB'— *Southern Cross'* radio call sign. He stayed awake and 'tuned in' for as long as his friend was in the air, the longest stretch being 33 hours during the Hawaii to Fiji leg.

More to the point, rival press outlets could also hear transmissions from *Southern Cross*, threatening the exclusive deals Ulm had signed with *The Sun* and *The LA Examiner*. In the evening, Warner received sharp messages from the owners of both newspapers claiming that Associated Press was reporting their messages freely. On Ulm's instructions, Warner broadcast a message warning operators not to pass the messages on to anyone other than their intended recipients. Ulm also sent a message

to the editors, apologising and reassuring them that the deals still stood. His broadcast to *The LA Examiner* illustrates how he continued to manage the business side of things even at 4,000 feet above the Pacific and reveals something of the charm he wielded in his business relationships.

> *TO 6ARD*
>
> *Personal to Eric Cullenward stop We dont break our word or violate contracts sorry you were troubled but same beyond my control will loyally serve Examiner until contract concluded stop Gee its great out here but apparently business worries even reach me here stop Smoke two cigarettes at once one for me Smithy and I both crave the odd smoke love and kisses cheerio*

Intending to control the story reported in the press and perhaps aware of Warner's nervous disposition, Ulm instructed his radio operator to only send messages that he had first approved. Nonetheless, Charlie Hodge's radio log indicates that throughout the flight both Americans slipped personal transmissions in between the 'official' ones ordered by Ulm. At 8.30 pm, for example, Ulm passed Warner a message to send:

> *Thirty eight hundred feet above endless miles of clouds. No stars or moon visible yet. Perfectly clear up here. No necessity go higher yet. Motors haven't missed a beat thanks to Maidment. Smith must be in love I can't make him eat. He's had three to my ten sandwiches to date. Stars are just coming up. Will send more later. Chas Ulm, Southern Cross.*

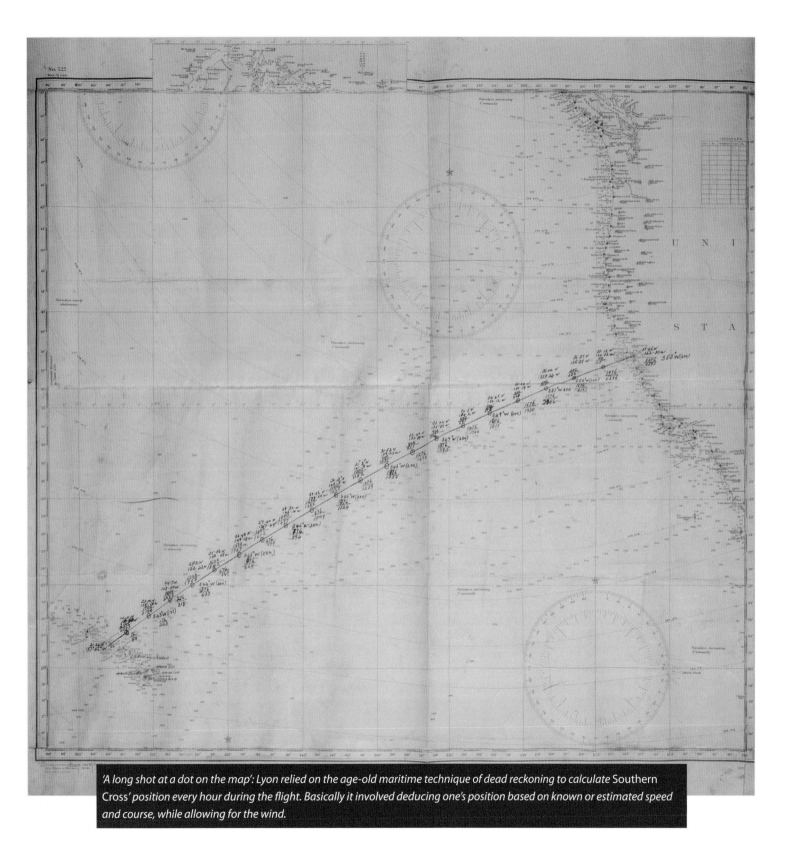

'A long shot at a dot on the map': Lyon relied on the age-old maritime technique of dead reckoning to calculate *Southern Cross'* position every hour during the flight. Basically it involved deducing one's position based on known or estimated speed and course, while allowing for the wind.

Harry the E. I. C. is now Centre, does it check up with the other Compasses if not better not use it but trust the aperiodic and this until you can get a sight.

'... "wise cracks" ad lib': The crew's reliance on passing notes allows us to eavesdrop on their conversations to gain an insight into both matters technical and the relationships between the crew.

'It's now a very small world we live in': The trans-Pacific flight foreshadowed the globilisation of transport, communications and the media.

Typical for a man of his generation and the same as his three comrades, Kingsford Smith smoked heavily. Abstaining for dozens of hours at a time provided one of the flight's most frequently mentioned discomforts.

To this, Warner added for his listeners on both sides of the Pacific:

> *The moon shining down is casting our shadow into the clouds with a great white circle around the faint shadow of the Southern Cross on the clouds. I'm sending this as I see it. Jim. Radio Opr.*

The addition of such striking descriptions and running commentaries would make Warner an object of great fascination to the Australian public. It was via his electronic 'voice', produced in the staccato rap of a brass key, that they could follow, in what we would call 'real time' *Southern Cross'* record-breaking journey. They, like us, have good reason to be thankful that he disregarded his employer's instructions and that he had such a patient and resilient friend in the United States Navy.

'Sailing lazily on the Milky Way'

To estimate the aircraft's drift and ground speed (which he needed to measure their position accurately) Lyon had a crude 'speed and drift indicator' bolted to the side of the fuselage, just outside the rear cabin door. This, as he explained in his memoirs, made it necessary for him 'to open the door to an angle of forty-five degrees and prop it so while I laid down on the floor, stuck my head out and manipulated the instrument'. Peering through it, he would measure the aircraft's speed and drift against objects on the ground, typically the white caps on waves. To provide a reference point in the dark, he had calcium flares that ignited on contact with the water. At 10 pm, he threw

some out. All eyes watched them—the only thing visible in the all-consuming darkness surrounding *Southern Cross*. 'They struck the water and burst into a white blaze and we watched them for about twenty minutes', wrote Kingsford Smith. Lyon followed them with his drift indicator, the violent slipstream outside the aircraft buffeting his head violently and occasionally causing the cabin door to slam shut, providing him with 'a most resounding thwack on the back of the head'. Perceiving 'a very slight drift to the southward' he accordingly provided Kingsford Smith with a revised heading on the Earth Inductor Compass.

During that first night's flying, the difficulty of Lyon's job was augmented by the fact that, since midday, Warner had been unable to pick up the Army radio beacon. Then, just before midnight, the artificial horizon on Lyon's sextant broke, preventing him from factoring astrological measurements into his dead reckoning until he could see the horizon again. Fortunately, around 1 am Warner made radio contact with a steamer, the *Maliko*. Assisted by a radio compass, its navigator informed Warner that *Southern Cross* was actually a few miles north of Lyon's estimated position. There was also some non-official banter between the crews, *Maliko's* captain being an old friend of Lyon's. On a scrap of paper, Warner passed on a message:

'Harry, how would a high ball go now?'

Lyon scribbled a reply and passed it back: 'Did Hansen say that? Tell Hansen fine.'

Lyon had three traditional magnetic compasses, such as this one, to check the EIC for errors.

Just before 2 am, Kingsford Smith spotted *Maliko* as 'some pinpoints of light' off to the port bow. He recalled how this, the first sign of life they had seen since leaving San Francisco 17 hours earlier, 'evoked [a] friendly feeling towards this only other occupant of the vast and dark space beneath us'. Ulm took control and circled the *Maliko* while Kingsford Smith signaled 'O.K.S.C.' with a spotlight.

Within 20 minutes Warner had pushed a note into the cockpit telling Ulm he had communicated with another vessel, the *Manoa*. Shortly afterwards, its lights appeared, glowing like 'minute points of fire' on the black void below. Although they had verified the location of several ships in the vicinity of their flight path before leaving San Francisco, these two vessels would be the only ones the crew would see during the entire flight to Australia.

The hours between midnight and dawn passed uneventfully, though uncomfortably. As Ulm and Kingsford Smith would have recalled from nights in the trenches at Gallipoli, the cold and bleary-eyed weariness of these hours had a habit of grinding on for what seemed an eternity. To fight the biting chill the two Australians pulled on flying overalls over their suits. Their American colleagues meanwhile made do with woollen sweaters.

The greatest hardship as those frigid hours crept by, however, was the almost unbearable desire for a cigarette. 'One would have been the summit of earthly felicity', admitted Ulm, though the frightening prospect of a fire in the aircraft compelled all the crew to suppress their cravings. As *Southern Cross* bore on through the night, Kingsford Smith and Ulm took turns stretching out in their deep wicker chairs for some 'fitful dozing' while Warner and Lyon did the same on the cabin floor. 'It had not occurred to me that I might easily get a little sleep', remembered Warner. He didn't feel tired, though: 'It was all too interesting'.

At 3.37 am the night's calm clarity ended and a rain squall closed in. Giving the engines 'the gun', Kingsford Smith climbed through sheets of rain, *Southern Cross* rocking and lurching in the disturbed air. Unable to see the horizon, he had to put complete faith in his instruments, watching them carefully to ensure he kept the lumbering aircraft above its stalling speed.

THE SUN, SUNDAY, JUNE 17, 1928

"Dearest Captain"

LETTERS
TO OUR AIR
HEROES

Kingsford Smith

C. T. P. Ulm

The publication of Ulm's log entries and wireless messages cultivated interest in the flight and endeared him and Kingsford Smith to the Australian public.

At 6,000 feet they burst out into bright, clear skies above the storm. Looking down, Ulm perceived an epic cloudscape, bathed in the moonlight. 'Moon on clouds; beautiful effect', he recorded in the log. 'Breaks in clouds look like rivers and canyons.' For *National Geographic*'s readers, Ulm would later expand on this to provide a lyrical impression of what he beheld that night 6,000 feet above the Pacific.

We gazed down from above into grim, grey cloud valleys, where the massive cloud cliffs glittered eerily under the moon. White cloud buttes stood out boldly like the ramparts of a giant Arctic berg. They broke into deep canyons; they hunched into mighty peaks and fell away into bewildering white foothills and plains. Down in those torturous ravines moonlight seemed to flow, scintillating like a trickling brook of melted silver. Dun cliffs crumpled, abysses closed, canyons were crushed, the silver rivers were lost, and a new cloud topography arose with every mile.

The moon cast *Southern Cross'* shadow onto the clouds, creating a 'ghost plane' that, in contrast to the real aircraft's steady course, plunged erratically into cloudy ravines and leaped up over soft, glowing peaks. In the hours before dawn, this surreal setting enthralled the four airmen. To their exhausted, chilled and noise-numbed minds, the soft white light and constantly, but almost imperceptibly, changing cloudscape gave the impression of a dream. 'There was no world', thought Ulm. 'We were sailing lazily on the Milky Way.'

'MAUNA KEA SIGHTED!'

Hawaii, 1 June 1928

4.45   Moon on clouds beautiful effect
Breaks in clouds look like rivers
and Canyons

          Alt. 6000 ft.
          Speed 73 knots
          Revs. 1600

5.55   Dawn breaks — Moon sets
we at 7500 feet

6.33   375 Nautical miles from Honolulu
       330   "   "   "   nearest land

6.43   Gliding down thro' clouds
now. 4800 ft. Speed 80 knots

6.54   Now at 3000 Speed 86 knots — Revs 1575
Oct   Going thro' some of the lower
Am   clouds.

6.57   2600 ft Speed in Glide 94 knots.
Revs 1575

4.45	Moon on clouds beautiful effect. Breaks in clouds look like rivers and canyons
	Alt 6000 ft
	Speed 73 knots
	Revs 1600
5.55	Dawn breaks—moon sets
	we at 7 500 feet
6.33	375 nautical miles from Honolulu
	330 " " " nearest land
6.43	Gliding down thru clouds now 4800 ft. Speed 80 knots
6.54 PCT am	Now at 3000. Speed 86 knots—Revs 1575. Going thro' some of the lower clouds.
6.57	2600 ft. Speed in glide 94 knots. Revs 1575

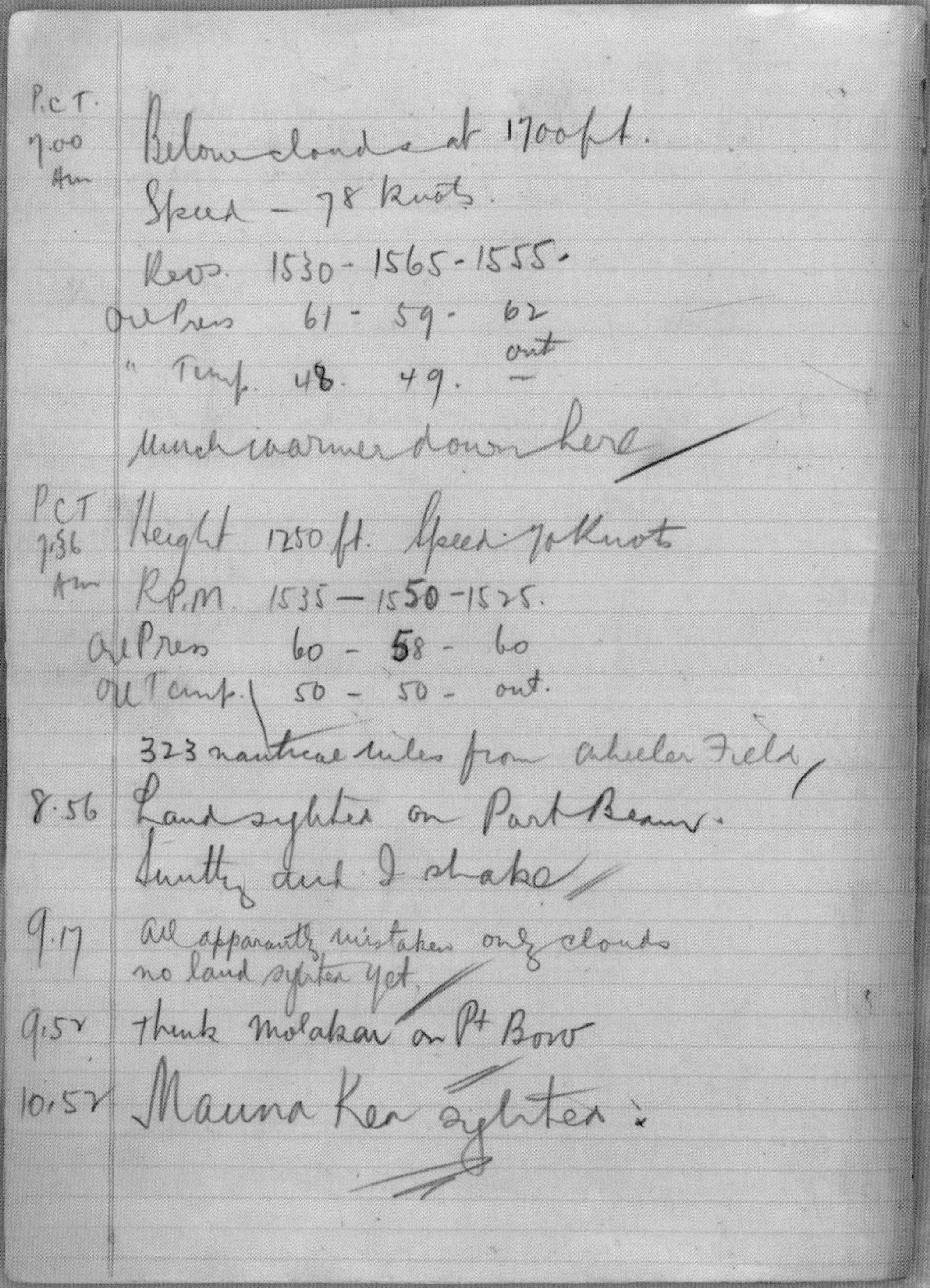

P.C.T.
7.00 Am — Below clouds at 1700 ft.

Speed — 78 knots.

Revs. 1530 - 1565 - 1555.

Oil Press 61 - 59 - 62

" Temp. 48. 49. out —

Much warmer down here

P.C.T.
7.36 Am — Height 1250 ft. Speed 90 knots

R.P.M. 1535 — 1550 - 1525.

Oil Press 60 - 58 - 60

Oil Temp. 50 - 50 - out.

323 nautical miles from Wheeler Field.

8.56 Land sighted on Port Beam.
Smithy and I shake

9.17 All apparently mistaken only clouds
no land sighted yet.

9.52 Think Molakai on Pt Bow

10.52 Mauna Kea sighted :

PCT 7.00 AM	Below clouds at 1700ft
	Speed—78 knots
	Revs 1530 – 1565 – 1555
	Oil Press 61 – 59 – 62
	" Temp 48 – 49 – out
	Much warmer down here
PCT 7.36 AM	Height 1250ft. Speed 70 knots
	RPM 1535 – 1550 – 1525
	Oil Press 60 – 58 – 60
	Oil Temp 50 – 50 – out
	323 nautical miles from Wheeler Field
8.56	Land sighted on Port Beam.
	Smithy and I shake
9.17	All apparently mistaken only clouds
	No land sighted yet
9.52	Think Molakai on Pt Bow
10.52	Mauna Kea sighted!

After 27 hours in the air, Southern Cross lands at Wheeler Field, the United States Air Force aerodrome on Oahu, 1 June 1928.

The crew spent the hours before dawn chilled numb, deaf from the engine noise and hovering on the edge of an exhausted daze. Eyes smarted and joints ached from cold and lack of use. Besides a smoke, everyone longed for the sun's warmth.

When dawn broke at 5.55 am, the epic, towering clouds they had been flying among for the last few hours vanished with the darkness, leaving a blanket of haze over the sea. As the sun came up, the crew had a breakfast of sandwiches and coffee, with, as Warner recalled, 'a vote of thanks to the inventor of Thermos bottles'. The hot drink and the sun's first rays did wonders for their frozen joints.

As the sun came up Kingsford Smith began a slow descent from 7,500 feet to get below the clouds where they could watch for land. They glided down through the overcast, hurried along by a tail wind, and levelled out at 1,250 feet above a leaden sea. Before losing sight of the last stars, Lyon took a sextant shot and calculated they were about 600 kilometres north-east of Wheeler Field, the United States Army Air Corps' aerodrome on Oahu. Even with the tail wind's help, they still had at least four hours' flying. Ulm's mind again turned to the fuel sloshing about in the tank behind them. He suspected the gauges of playing up but wasn't sure. They might only have enough to keep the engines going for three hours, a speculation he noted and passed through to the Americans.

Just before 9 am, exactly 24 hours after take-off, something on the horizon caught Ulm's eye. He turned to the back of the log and scribbled a note to Kingsford Smith: 'First sight of land?' (see page 168). The two men gripped each other in a triumphant handshake and passed a note through to the cabin sharing the news. Peering out the port window, Lyon spotted what appeared to be a small, rocky island, something that with almost five years' sailing in these waters he failed to recognise. Despite the muggy, tropical air, Lyon immediately went cold. 'I began to wonder if I had passed the island of Kauai ... The sensation of having missed my landfall (Molokai channel) was sickening.' Consulting his charts, Lyon concluded that the island Ulm had spotted lay on the western edge of the Hawaiian group, putting *Southern Cross* some 240 kilometres beyond its destination.

Warner, already nervous about Ulm's latest fuel calculations, immediately discerned the bewilderment on Lyon's face. He passed the navigator a note asking if they were lost, on which Lyon replied with an unequivocal 'YES'. Panic gripped Warner, causing him to soil his pants. Hastily he transmitted 'Guess we are lost' and requested all listeners to tune in on his frequency. Land-based operators relayed the message and commercial stations began interrupting their programs with dramatic newsflashes.

But Warner had reacted prematurely. Even as he was transmitting, Lyon was taking a

A pair of wind-driven generators powered Southern Cross' *wireless equipment. The port-side unit played up consistently, leaving Warner unable to receive transmissions for large stages of the journey.*

sextant shot and recalculating their position. The results conformed to the course he had been plotting all night, putting them east of Hawaii and still well out of sight of any land. Perplexed, he passed a note through to the cockpit asking Kingsford Smith to change course for the island. As they did so, Warner began to consider the Dole fliers who had perished in these waters. 'I wondered if they had become uneasy and started changing course at random, which could easily have been the case.'

Twenty-two minutes after their exuberant handshake, Kingsford Smith and Ulm saw the 'island' suddenly dissolve before their eyes. It had been a cloud, an optical illusion accentuated by their altitude and the dull, overcast conditions. To reassure himself, Lyon asked Warner to request a confirmation of their position from Hawaiian radio stations via the bearing of *Southern Cross'* radio signal. With almost no power left for the receiver— the port generator for recharging the battery having failed—and practically deaf from the engine noise, Warner just managed to make out a transmission from Hilo station on Hawaii's east coast. It fixed their bearing relative to the station, matching Lyon's dead reckoning to within a few kilometres. 'It was gratifying to find out that I was right on my calculations', explained the navigator.

Kingsford Smith returned *Southern Cross* to its original course and everyone resumed their vigil, scanning the horizon for land. Over the next two hours, clouds continued to play tricks, Ulm recalling that 'we nudged each other at least a dozen times to look at some dark shadow that appeared to be "the real thing"'. Although the others seem to have been reassured by the vindication of Lyon's navigational skills, Warner remained badly shaken. Contrary to Ulm's instructions, between 10 am and 11 am he transmitted an almost constant stream of messages, painting a grim picture for radio listeners.

> *Just can stay up for 4 hours more … Our 'A' batteries down. Can't receive anything … These clouds everywhere we turn … only got one more hour gas now … Wonder if you're getting me now. Tell Uncle Sammy to keep them destroyers leased … I mite have swimming exercise yet … These clouds are deceiving … stay with us.*

Warner's son Tom believed that his father 'began sending just anything so that several ships, or, stations, could obtain a bearing on them and then triangulate their position'. Charlie Hodge, anxiously listening from USS *Omaha*'s radio room agreed, attributing it to 'keen headwork' by Warner. Nonetheless, it appears the other crew members remained much more sanguine throughout the morning. Always eager to emphasise the diligence of their preparations and skill, Ulm and Kingsford Smith later vehemently denied they were ever 'lost'.

Shortly before 11 am, Kingsford Smith climbed to 4,500 feet to extend the range of their observation. As he did, Ulm spotted 'a brown bulge … a domelike island rising from a vast ocean of vapor' off the port bow. Seeing it too, Lyon consulted his charts and confirmed that it was the 13,796-foot peak of Mauna Kea, a volcano on the island of Hawaii. The jubilance this inspired reverberates through the scrap-paper notes that changed hands between the cockpit and cabin in the following moments.

> *Damned good work Harry, old Lion. Keep on doing your stuff—Smithy and Chas.*
>
> *If we get a cigarette and a cup of coffee we'll feel like flying back—ha, what, Old Top. [Lyon]*

Half an hour later, *Southern Cross* was above the eastern fringe of the Hawaiian Islands with Maui and Molokai in sight, as Ulm recalled, 'purple and gleaming in the sunlight'. Beyond them lay Oahu which Lyon reckoned 'most beautiful' in the morning sun. As they approached it sugar plantations emerged 'like huge lawns', making the whole island appear 'so green and fresh'. Over Diamond Head, a formation of United States Army Air Corps aircraft circled, waiting to escort them in.

Even with their destination in sight, Warner remained on the verge of panic. To his anxious listeners he reported that they could see land but anticipated that it would be 'a race whether we make it to landing or not before fuel is exhausted'. The radio's dying batteries added dramatic tension, creating large gaps between his transmissions. USS *Omaha*'s radio room was packed with sailors, all gripped by the drama. 'Minutes seem like hours to me now', noted Warner's old friend Charlie Hodge. 'But I bet it is days to Jim up there about out of gas and water so close!'

At a few minutes past noon (10 am Hawaiian time), *Southern Cross* passed low over Honolulu to, as one reporter described, 'whistles and bells, and the jubilant shouts of thousands in the streets'. Twelve minutes later, Kingsford Smith eased the aircraft onto Wheeler Field, the wheels touching down 27 hours and 23 minutes after leaving the ground at Oakland. Kingsford Smith switched off the engines, the abrupt silence leaving everyone on board, in his words, 'blank and wondering what had happened'.

About 15,000 people had gathered at the airfield; reports of Warner's radio transmissions over a loud speaker had built tension to an almost unbearable level. Now, as the airmen emerged from *Southern Cross*, dazed and dishevelled, the crowd erupted in pent-up excitement. 'As I stepped out of the machine', recollected Kingsford Smith, 'I caught sight of a sea of faces advancing on me from every

direction. The next moment we were swallowed up'. People swarmed around, bombarding them with questions they struggled to understand with their noise-fatigued ears. Kingsford Smith caught one from a young lady, who wanted to know if they had been afraid they wouldn't make it: 'Hell, no, Madam, I was born to be hanged not drowned'.

Police ushered the airmen, adorned in traditional flower leis, to an official welcoming party consisting of the Dole Air Race winners, Art Goebel and William Davis, and Captain Lowell Smith, who in 1924 had circumnavigated the northern hemisphere by air. Also waiting to welcome the weary fliers were the Hawaiian Governor and Major Henry Miller, commander of Wheeler Field and a man whose assistance they would rely on heavily to prepare for the next stage. Surrounding the podium, in Ulm's words, jostled a horde of journalists with the 'most formidable battery of cameras' he had ever seen.

After a round of speeches that nobody heard above the noise of the crowd, cars whisked the aviators off to the Royal Hawaiian Hotel at Waikiki where the manager had insisted they stay as his guests. Before retiring for much-needed sleep they faced another 'battery of movie cameras' in front of the hotel. Warner and Lyon, remembering the contract, sought Ulm's permission before speaking to any journalists. Following breakfast, the four airmen turned in to sleep for the rest of the day.

Kingsford Smith walks from Southern Cross with American pilot Art Goebel (right), winner of the 1927 Dole Air Race. Like Kingsford Smith, Goebel came to flying during the Great War and afterwards worked in the Hollywood film industry.

The trans-Pacific flight catapulted Lyon and Warner from anonymity into the ranks of America's pioneering airmen.

Southern Cross remained at Wheeler Field overnight in the care of the United States Army Air Corps. Its mechanics went over the machine carefully, repairing a damaged cylinder on the starboard engine and the faulty generator that had failed to keep the wireless receiver's battery charged. Ulm had instructed them to drain the fuel tanks so he could see how accurate his calculations had been. Had it been a critically close-run thing? Were Warner's dramatic wireless messages warranted? From *Southern Cross'* tanks, air force mechanics collected almost 500 litres, enough for another three hours' flying.

'Dramatic story from the sky'

Southern Cross arrived in Honolulu at 6.17 am on 2 June, Sydney time. It was perfect timing for an afternoon newspaper like *The Sun;* the front page of that afternoon's edition carried accounts from a correspondent in Honolulu as well as radio messages transmitted by Warner during the night.

It was the following day, however, that *The Sun* featured the real scoop. After sleeping throughout the afternoon, Ulm wired the contents of his log to the newspaper's offices, as per the contract he and Kingsford Smith had signed. Under the headline 'Dramatic story from the sky—fliers' own narrative—diary penned in the clouds', *The Sun* presented a narrative of the Oakland–Honolulu leg in Ulm's words. Interestingly, the newspaper edited it to imply that Kingsford Smith was the author. Indeed, *The Sun*'s initial coverage on 3 June established a precedent for his dominance in the history of the Pacific flight and laid the foundations for the so-called 'Smithy' legend. In several pages of stories devoted to the flight, Ulm and the Americans barely rated a mention. *The Sun*'s journalists interviewed Kingsford Smith's parents, conveying stories of his background that would later become integral to 'Smithy' folklore. Catherine and William Kingsford Smith

related the story, for example, of young 'Chilla' leaping from the roof of their Longueville home as a five-year-old in an early attempt at flight. Meanwhile, the other newspapers had to make do with far less impressive second-hand reports from syndicated correspondents, justifying *The Sun*'s £1,000 investment for exclusive access to the fliers.

Before the flight, the mood of Australian newspapers towards the airmen had cooled, with some even criticising their preparations and lack of experience. Upon their arrival in Honolulu, however, this immediately changed to unadulterated acclaim. The press

The relief in being back on terra firma is written all over Warner's face. To his left stands fellow American Martin Jensen who claimed second place in the Dole competition.

immediately cast the flight as one of great national and historical significance and the airmen as a new breed of pioneer. *The Sun's* editor, for example, proclaimed *Southern Cross'* safe arrival on Oahu as symbolic of national triumph and evidence of greatness in the Australian character. He pointed out that although the venture had originated in the United States, a country with some 20 times the population of Australia, its organisation and execution were entirely the work of Australians. This was hardly surprising, though, suggested the editor, as the flight merely resulted from the lingering pioneering spirit. 'Whenever there is a chance of adventure', he trumpeted, 'there is apt to be an Australian not far away'. At this stage the Australian press had only a vague conception of the extent of American involvement in the flight. George Allan Hancock's remarkably generous offer to finance the flight after Australian governments withdrew support had not been publicly announced, and the crucial support of the United States military, both before and during the flight, was yet to properly figure in the dispatches of correspondents. These things would be revealed in the coming days and acknowledged by the Australian press, though they would do little to alter the prevailing view at the time and since, that *Southern Cross'* triumph was an Australian one.

Press coverage of the trans-Pacific flight established Kingsford Smith as a dominant figure in Australian popular culture and an enduring emblem of nationalist sentiment. Despite having engineered the publicity, Ulm received far less attention.

THE SUN

No. 5481   (Registered at the General Post Office, Sydney,)   SYDNEY : SATURDAY, JUNE 2, 1928   'Phones: B6021 to B6029

Honolulu Gives Rousing Welcome to Southern Cross

"THE OIL"

MILLIONAIRE BACKER

HAD PILOTED 'PLANE

"REAL CHANCE" AT LAST

("Sun" Special)

SAN FRANCISCO, Friday.

A leading retired capitalist, of Los Angeles, Mr. G. Allen Hancock, the special representative of "The Sun" has learned, is financially backing the flight of the Southern Cross.

As owner of the Santa Maria railway and of the La Brea Oil Company,

Anxious watchers wait all night for the airmen to arrive.

Mr. Hancock is one of the richest men in Southern California. He has given much time and money to scientific explorations, some of which were conducted in his own vessel. Greatly interested in aviation, he piloted the Southern Cross on its last trip north.

Shortly before the hop-off yesterday, Captain Kingsford Smith gave

LAST HOUR THRILLS

LOST, WANDERED, FOUND, TRIUMPHED

DINNER IN THE DARK

WHEN "GANG" STOPPED SMOKING

("Sun" Special)

HONOLULU, Friday.

The distant hum of rhythmic motors was heard, and then a tiny speck emerged from the eastern sky. It rapidly grew larger, and swooped gracefully earthwards. It was the Southern Cross.

Captain Kingsford Smith and his intrepid companions had completed the first great stage of their epoch-making flight across the Pacific.

They had a tumultuous welcome, for the relief was tremendous.

The 'plane landed at Wheeler Field aerodrome at 9.49 a.m. (Honolulu time), equal to 12.19 p.m. (San Francisco time), and to 6.19 a.m., Saturday (Sydney time). This made their actual flying time 27 hours 25 minutes for 2091 miles.

Captain Kingsford Smith says, that, as far as he knows, the Southern Cross can hop off for Fiji on Sunday.

The visibility from Wheeler Field was excellent, the bold promontory of Diamond Head looming clearly to the approaching fliers.

Cheer after cheer went up from the field, where a vociferous welcome was led by Governor Farrington and other

"No; we are not weary," he said to Governor Farrington, who pushed forward to greet him.

"The San Francisco radio beacon kept us going in wonderful shape for the first 400 miles."

The leader himself was at the con-

asked: "Were you ever afraid you wouldn't make Hawaii?"

"Hell, no, Madam," he replied, "I was born to be hanged, not drowned."

He added that the engine performed perfectly. All three motors never missed fire from start to finish.

up practically all night listening to the radios from Kingsford Smith and sending back encouraging messages.

Six ships had steam up ready to dash seaward in case an accident befell the Southern Cross as she approached Honolulu.

SYDNEY LISTENS

The Southern Cross is making wireless as well as flying history.

Never before has Australia been able to follow a trans-oceanic flight almost mile by mile. A continuous watch during the 29 hours that passed from the time that the 'plane left San Francisco till it reached Honolulu was kept at the Amalgamated Wireless station at La Perouse, and the messages received were telephoned to "The Sun."

Last night the messages were broadcast from 2SL, so that listeners-in were able to follow the flight. Strangely enough, it was only when the 'plane was over the island of Oahu, and almost at its destination, that the messages faded out.

9.20 p.m., 1100 miles south-west of San Francisco: "A steady flame is flowing out of the exhaust pipe. The Wright Whirlwind motors are doing their duty loyally. Harry Lyon is now shooting at a star. The motors have not missed one beat. Everything is perfect. There is no necessity to go high yet."—Kingsford Smith.

Warner In Bumps

10 p.m.: "Station K.O.G., Honolulu is now communicating with us. The gang in the rear cockpit has started smoking. Smithy stopped because of the normal overflow of petrol there.—Ulm."

1200 miles out: "Our speed is 75 knots and altitude 4000 feet. We have been talking to Maliko and just passed through a pocket and dropped down a bit. It is Warner's first experience of flying. Every time we hit a bump he grabs the sides, but manages to laugh."

The Sun *breaks the story of* Southern Cross' *arrival in Honolulu on the afternoon of 2 June 1928.*

'ON THE WAY AND HAPPY'

Bound for Suva, 2–3 June 1928

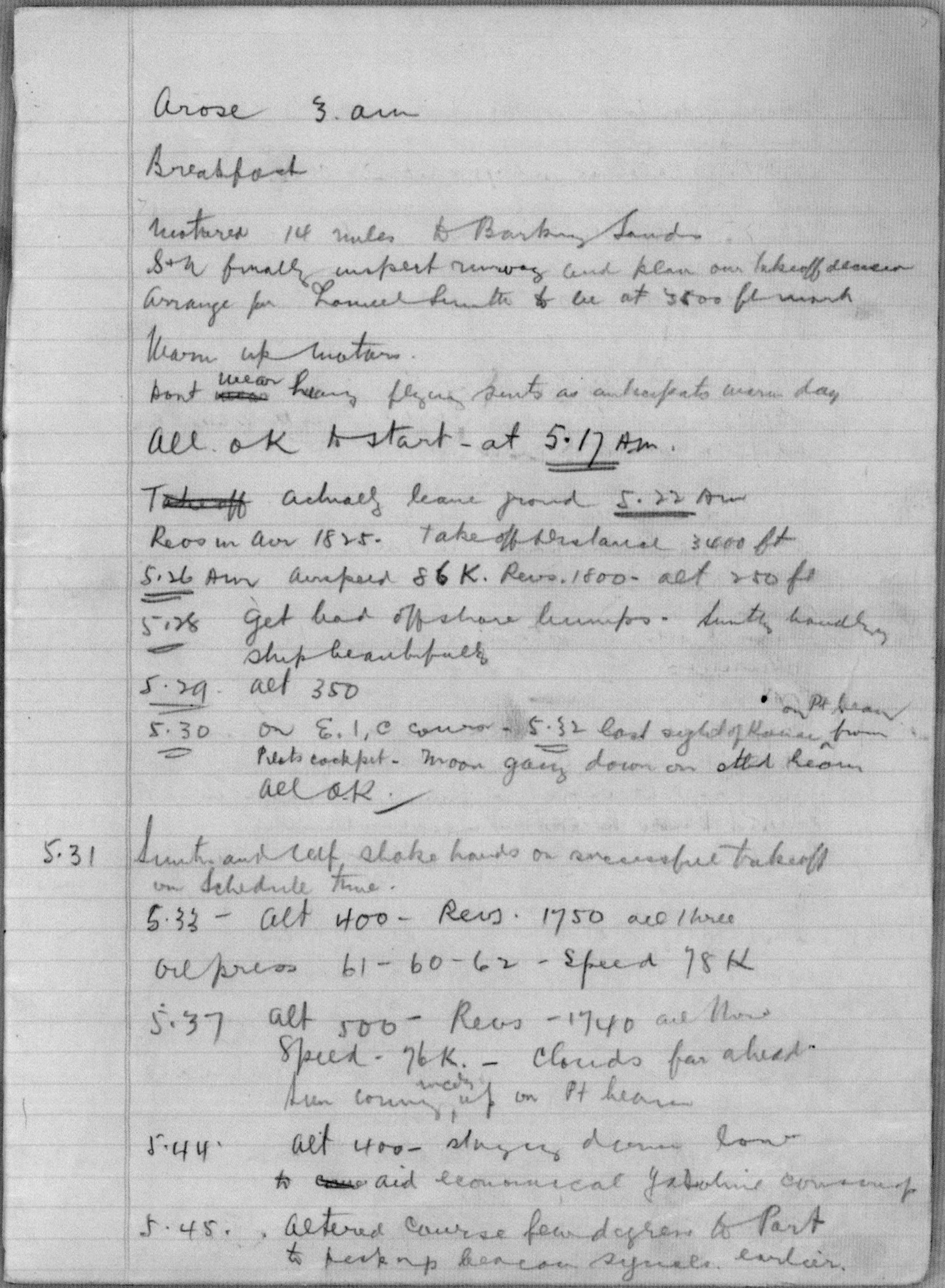

Arose 3. am

Breakfast

Motored 14 miles to Barking Sands
S+U finally inspect runway and plan our takeoff distance
Arrange for Launcel hunter to be at 3500 ft mark

Warm up motors.
Dont ~~wear~~ heavy flying suits as anticipate warm day

All. ok to start - at 5·17 Am.

~~Takeoff~~ actually leave ground 5·22 Am
Revs in Air 1825. Takeoff distance 3400 ft
5·26 Am Airspeed 86 K. Revs. 1800 - alt 250 ft
5·28 Get bad offshore bumps - Smithy handling
ship beautifully
5·29 alt 350
5·30 on E.1,C course - 5·32 lost sight of Hawaii from ·on Pt beam
Pilots cockpit - Moon going down on Stbd beam
alt o.k.

5·31 Smithy and Ulf shake hands on successful takeoff
on Schedule time.
5·33 - alt 400 - Revs. 1750 all three
oil press 61 - 60 - 62 - Speed 78 K
5·37 alt 500 - Revs - 1740 all three
Speed - 76 K. - Clouds far ahead.
Sun coming up on Pt beam
5·44· alt 400 - staying down low
to ~~aid~~ aid economical gasoline consumption
5·45· Altered course few degrees to Port
to pickup beacon signals earlier.

Arose 3.am

Breakfast

Motored 14 miles to Barking Sands.

S + U finally inspect runway and plan our takeoff decision.
Arrange for Lowell Smith to be at 3500 ft mark.

Warm up motors.

Dont wear heavy flying suits and anticipate warm day

All OK to start at 5.17 AM

~~Takeoff~~ Actually leave ground at 5.22 AM

Revs in air 1825. Take off distance 3400 ft

5.26 AM airspeed 86 k. Revs 1800. Alt 250 ft

5.28   get bad offshore bumps. Smithy handles ship beautifully

5.29   alt 350

5.30   On E.I.C course—5.32 last sight of Kauai on Pt beam
from pilots cockpit. Moon going down on stbd beam all
OK.

5.31   Smithy and self shake hands on successful takeoff on
schedule time

5.33   – alt 400 – Revs 1750 all three

Oil press 61 – 60 – 62 – Speed 78 k

5.37   Alt 500 – Revs – 1740 all three

Speed 76 k—Clouds far ahead.

Sun coming nicely up on Pt beam

5.44   alt 400—staying down low to aid economical gasoline
consumption

5.45   Altered course few degrees to Port to pick up beacon
signals earlier

5.50   Warner asks for more altitude that he may
let down long aerial / open up motor to
1775 Revs climbing at 75 knots — Clouds ahead
but think we can safely fly under them — Would
rather not fly blind so heavily loaded

5.58   Alt 850 - Revs 1710 - Speed 74 K.   Warner
reports quote one generator bad unquote this is
a little worrying as Radio was such
a wonderful aid to our previous flight — Both generators
appear to be running o.k.

6. am   Well we are on the way and happy,
alt 950 and now passing under low clouds with
sun ahead —

6.11   Picked up "A" beacon signals / This very
cheering —

6.17   Lyon sent me message reading quote Australia
the Shftr the Southern Cross and Mrs Lyons son Harry are
saved as I have found my missing papers unquote.
I didn't know he lost them.
Revs. 1700 Speed 74 K. alt 675 — on Beacon all o.k,

6.32   I am going to rest for an hour or so then
give Smith a rest at the controls

6.52   Self make first rough check on Gas
consumption — Believe seems better
than on Previous hop — this due to our
keeping lower altitude - Air Speed now
76 K - Est Gd Speed 84 K. Revs 1750 - Alt 850

5.50	Warner asks for more altitude that he may let down long wave aerial. Open up motors to 1775 Revs climbing at 75 knots—clouds ahead but think we can safely fly under them—would rather not fly blind so heavily loaded.
5.50	Alt 850 – Revs 1710 – Speed 74 K. Warner reports quote one generator bad unquote this is a little worrying as Radio was ~~been~~ such a wonderful aid to our previous flight. Both generators appear to be running OK.
6am	Well ~~we're~~ we are on the way and happy. Alt 900 and now passing under low clouds with more ahead—
6.11	Picked up "A" beam signals. This very cheering—
6.17	Lyon sent me message reading quote Australia United States the Southern Cross and Mrs Lyons son Harry are saved as I have found my missing papers unquote. I didnt know he lost them.
	Revs 1700 Speed 74 K. Alt 625—on Beacon all OK.
6.32	I am going to rest for hour or so then give Smithy a rest at the controls
6.52	~~Smith and self~~ make first rough check on gas consumption—Believe same better than on Previous hop—This due to our keeping lower altitude. Air speed now 76 K. Est Gd. Speed 84k. Revs 1750 – alt 850.

The Wright Aeronautical Corporation was among many businesses that used its association with the flight for advertising.

'Hectic' would be an apt word to describe Saturday 2 June 1928 for the four trans-Pacific fliers. Ulm envisaged leaving Hawaii the following day, his goal: 'Dinner in Sydney [next] Saturday night'. They had 24 hours therefore to prepare for the 5,000-kilometre journey to Fiji, the longest ocean flight anyone had ever attempted.

There was much to do if they were to keep Ulm's dogmatic schedule. Although Wheeler Field had been suitable as a landing ground, it lacked the runway length for *Southern Cross* to take off with a full load of fuel. A year before, Keith Anderson had reconnoitered alternative airstrips, recommending a beach on the neighbouring island of Kauai known as Barking Sands. Before the day's end, Ulm needed to arrange for the move of *Southern Cross* and almost 5,000 litres of fuel to Barking Sands and organise preparation of a 4,500-foot-long runway there. The Americans, meanwhile, had to repair some essential navigational tools that had failed during the first leg. It is little wonder then, that in his dispatches to *The Sun* that evening from Kauai, Ulm would explain, 'This has been the busiest day of my life'.

In the 5,000 kilometres of open ocean between the Hawaiian and Fijian islands there were few places *Southern Cross* might land in an emergency. Ulm had, however, recognised

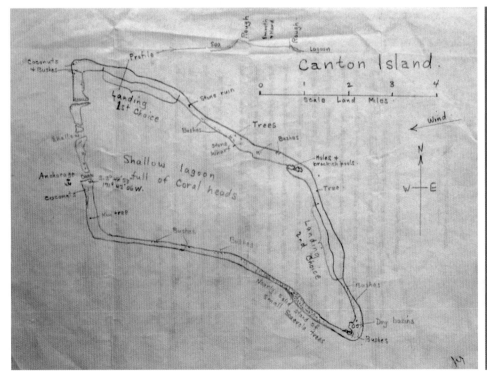

'A desperate, last ditch option': Ulm consulted the curators of the Bishop Museum and made sketches of islands in the Phoenix Group, on which Southern Cross might land in an emergency.

that their course passed close to the Phoenix islands. He visited the Bernice P. Bishop Museum in Honolulu, home to an impressive collection relating to Polynesian and Hawaiian culture, and spoke to curators with first-hand knowledge of the waters they would be crossing the following day. They suggested that the most suitable landing places might be on the islands of Canton and Enderbury. Although the presence of these islands along the planned flight path must have provided a sense of security, in reality they only represented a desperate, last-ditch option. Canton, which Ulm considered the more suitable of the pair for landing, was in fact a coral atoll ringing an immense lagoon. Enderbury was 5 kilometres long, but covered by palm trees, ponds and rocky outcrops. Landing on either island in the middle of the night, with nothing but moonlight to illuminate their deserted surfaces, appears an incredibly unlikely proposition. If the crew survived a forced landing, there would be no fresh water or help for hundreds of kilometres and no hope of getting *Southern Cross* off the ground again.

In the late afternoon, the crew flew from Wheeler Field to Barking Sands accompanied by Captain Lowell Smith and a team of eight Army mechanics in another Fokker. 'We were agreeably surprised at the condition of the runway', explained Ulm. Gangs of workmen had cleared and smoothed a 1,400-metre-long section of the beach, and the Army had stockpiled enough fuel there to fill *Southern Cross*' tanks to capacity. 'It has been hard work

to keep to my schedule', noted Ulm in the log. 'Unforeseen delays crop up; but Army and Navy co-operation splendidly helped us out.' Indeed, without the logistical support of the United States military, this Australian triumph would not, as it were, have made it off the ground in Hawaii.

Kauai had only five white residents, but typically, Lyon knew one of them. He stayed with this old friend that night and, from Warner's description of him attempting to rehydrate himself from a huge water jug at dawn the following morning, it appears he indulged in a heavy drinking session. The others stayed with the family of plantation owner Lindsay Faye at Kekaha, about 20 kilometres from Barking Sands. They had baths ('our first shave since we left Oakland', logged Ulm) and then dinner, which merged into 'hours of conference'.

Ulm, no doubt, probed every aspect of the planning to ensure that they had attended to every detail. He noted in the log how he and Kingsford Smith agreed to take the maximum amount of fuel possible. What he did not record, however, was the rather pessimistic arithmetic that had led them to this decision. As Kingsford Smith's biographer, Ian Mackersey, points out, Fiji lay 1,200 kilometres further from Hawaii than Oakland, yet they could only 'squeeze' enough additional fuel to extend their endurance for three hours or so. Despite warnings from several quarters in Hawaii that day, Ulm and Kingsford Smith refused to acknowledge the almost impossible odds with which this presented them and call off the flight.

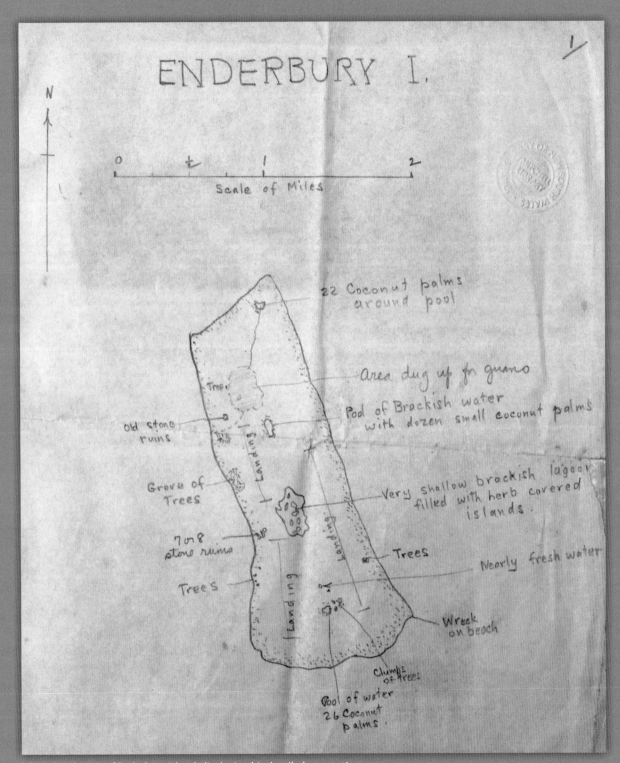

Ulm's sketch map of Enderbury Island, displaying his detailed annotation.

'A long shot at a dot on the map ...'

When the crew climbed aboard *Southern Cross* just after 5 am the following morning, Kingsford Smith recalled that it was a 'warm and rather muggy morning; the air was still, the sea calm, and the moon was bright'.

Kingsford Smith started *Southern Cross'* engines at 5.10 am, causing a cloud of the beach's white sand to engulf the aircraft. The small party of Army mechanics gathered to see them off. While the engines warmed for ten minutes, the crew checked over their equipment and provisions. In preparation for this, the Pacific crossing's longest leg, *Southern Cross* carried close to its maximum lifting power: almost 5 tonnes of fuel and oil and enough sustenance (48 sandwiches and a little under 4 litres of water and coffee each) to see them through the 36-hour flight. No wonder Kingsford Smith was aghast when Lyon turned up with a rubber life raft, loaned by his Navy friends. 'He refused to take it. Far too much weight', recalled Lyon. 'I think he even begrudged the weight of my sextant.'

At 5.20 am, Kingsford Smith opened up the throttles. Lowell Smith stood just over 1,000 metres further down the beach marking the point at which they needed to clear the ground. Not far beyond him, the beach curved, creating a drop-off into the sea. After running 900 metres, *Southern Cross'* wheels left the ground for a moment but then dropped

back into the sand. With just 100 metres to go, Kingsford Smith used the force to 'bounce' the aircraft off the end of the beach. In the back, Warner and Lyon felt their guts

This early-twentieth century example of a mariner's sextant would have been familiar to Lyon. His was only slightly modified by the addition of a spirit level to estimate the horizon's position.

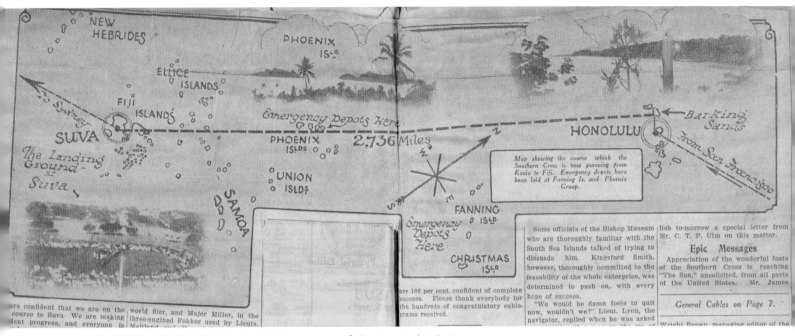

The flight from Barking Sands to Suva: the longest ocean flight attempted at the time.

churn as *Southern Cross* reached the top of its bound and dropped 25 feet before levelling out just above the surf.

Southern Cross could only manage the most gradual climb, taking five minutes to reach 300 feet. Coastal gusts rocked the overloaded aircraft violently, causing some anxious moments for all on board: any loss of control at that altitude would be fatal. Within ten minutes, Kauai disappeared over the horizon. 'All OK', recorded Ulm in the log. While Kingsford Smith and Ulm shared a now traditional handshake, Warner nervously passed a note to Lyon. 'Is he purposely flying at 100 ft or is she too heavy?' To conserve fuel Kingsford Smith and Ulm had agreed to fly as low as possible throughout this leg and, as Ulm

logged, 'Would rather not fly blind so heavily loaded'. At Warner's request Kingsford Smith coaxed *Southern Cross* a little higher so he could deploy the radio aerial.

The Oakland to Honolulu leg had been a significant achievement, but as Kingsford Smith later admitted, other aviators had flown that route before. The flight to Suva, however, took them into 'the unknown'. It made him nervous, but he also took great pride in the fact, perceiving himself as part of a lineage of Pacific explorers such as Balboa, Magellan and Bligh. 'I felt that we were following in the footsteps of these great predecessors and that we could claim kinship with them. They had traversed virgin waters; we were about to traverse virgin air.'

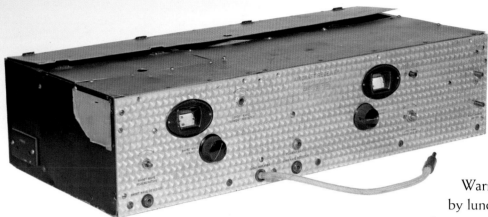

Southern Cross' *radio receiver, manufactured by Heintz and Kaufman in San Francisco.*

the rest of the morning with the radio set in pieces on the cabin floor rewiring it to run off the single working battery. Despite the turbulence and incessant engine vibration, Warner had the radio operating by lunchtime, though on only one battery it would remain practically incapable of receiving. 'We missed the chats with the world', Ulm and Kingsford Smith would later admit. 'With every mile the loss of the radio words became greater. Our sense of loneliness increased.'

Throughout the morning, pilot and co-pilot took shifts for an hour or so each at the controls. Flying conditions were ideal, the early overcast giving way to a bright, warm day. Just after 7 am as monotony began to settle in, Ulm spotted liquid on one of the fuel pipes above Kingsford Smith's head. He nudged his partner and pointed. As Kingsford Smith later explained, 'the possibilities were too dreadful to contemplate—the risk of a serious loss of petrol was only exceeded by the risk of a disastrous fire mid-ocean'. Ulm took the controls while Kingsford Smith reached up and dabbed his gloved finger into the liquid. Putting it to his lips, he grinned: just condensation. The relief must have been immense, though as Kingsford Smith admitted, 'the incident passed, but the memory of it remained with us for some time'.

As it had with their intrepid forebears, navigation weighed heavily on the margin separating succcess and failure. As Kingsford Smith described it, they were attempting 'a long shot at a dot on the map ... over 3000 miles away', with practically no landmarks by which to check their position. The United States Army rotated their radio beacon on Hawaii to face Suva, which should have provided Warner with the reassuring 'T' signal for about the first thousand kilometres of their flight. Just half an hour after take-off, however, Warner passed a note to the cockpit reporting 'one generator bad'. This, logged Ulm, was 'a little worrying' given the usefulness of radio navigation during the first leg.

Warner continued receiving the beacon for a time, but a little after 8 am lost the signal altogether. Soon after, the port generator failed, shorting out the receiver's battery. He spent

At least the petrol scare probably helped the aviators rein in their tobacco cravings by reinforcing the danger of smoking on board. There was the risk as the flight wore on and their confidence mounted, that they might become complacent about such things. Lyon, in fact, had demonstrated this tendency earlier in the morning when Warner broke a cigar in two and gave him half to chew. Soon afterwards, Warner was horrified to see Lyon produce a match and light his half: 'I pointed and waved and finally shook my fist at him before he came out of it and threw it overboard'. As he well knew, 'We had enough gas aboard to make a lovely explosion'.

Throughout the morning Lyon's dead reckoning indicated their excellent ground speed, the result of a tail wind that whipped them along at almost 167 kilometres per hour. Less promising was the sky ahead. As the morning wore on, the firm, clear line of the horizon became blurred with haze and then obscured by cloud. By 11.40 am dense rain clouds hung low over the ocean, right on their course. As they flew into the storm, the wind picked up, rocking Southern Cross gently at first but soon bouncing it violently in the turbulence.

Kingsford Smith skirted around the first cloudburst and then passed the controls to Ulm so he could navigate about the outskirts of another. Within moments, tropical thunderstorms were 'closing in all round'. Kingsford Smith took the controls while Ulm kept a running commentary in the log. 'He has just seen a way through, and we may miss them … Here they are again—all round us.' Pushing the three throttle leavers forward, Kingsford Smith pulled the control wheel back, causing Southern Cross to struggle up through the torrents of rain. 'Running into these storms when only 600 feet and heavily loaded is no joke … what bumps.' At 1,000 feet they emerged from the cloud barely above stalling speed and in a murky, grey haze between towering storm-clouds. 'More ahead', scribbled Ulm. 'Visibility only about 200 feet—ceiling nil.' Kingsford Smith pushed the wheel forward, hoping to make it underneath the 'menacing black curtain of water' ahead. Ulm reckoned the wind gusts buffeted them from three directions.

Five minutes later they were back at 600 feet and emerging into clearer weather. It suddenly became stifling in the cabin: everyone began removing clothing to cope with the tropical heat. Warner recalled how throughout the afternoon after each radio update he would remove an article of clothing until he sat at his radio set in his singlet and underwear. The increase in temperature and the storms is not surprising as by 12.45 pm, Lyon's dead reckoning put them 1,166 kilometres from Kauai and on the verge of the 'Intertropical Front'. This weather band (known nowadays as the Intertropical Convergence Zone) runs around the earth to the north of the equator during the northern hemisphere summer. The convergence of northern and southern trade winds produces a curtain of ferocious thunderstorms across the Pacific.

At this time of year the band could straddle a particularly wide area of the central Pacific. For the rest of the afternoon, Kingsford Smith and Ulm flew an erratic course attempting to dodge one thunderstorm after another. Those they could not fly around, they ploughed on through, each time enduring several minutes of blind flying through a 'dim, opaque world of nothingness'. Already doubting the sufficiency of their fuel supply, they agreed not to climb above the weather. By mid-afternoon the seals around *Southern Cross'* windshield had loosened. Half an hour later Kingsford Smith and Ulm were drenched.

Handling the heavy, unwieldy aircraft in such turbulent weather was exhausting work. Its rudder in particular required an immense amount of leg strength to operate. Kingsford Smith and Ulm took turns throughout the afternoon. At 3.30 pm, Ulm had just completed a tough hour at the wheel when the starboard motor gave 'a tremendous cough … followed by a splutter and a kick'. Everyone's heart skipped a beat: the engine resumed, but then coughed again. A note appeared on the stick from Warner and Lyon asking what was happening.

Ulm inspected the fuel lines but found nothing wrong. The two airmen exchanged scribbled hypotheses, Ulm suggesting rainwater had found its way into the carburettor stoves. After eight minutes of intermittent splutters, the starboard engine resumed its infinitely reassuring drone. Checking the gauges and seeing that they registered no problems, Ulm dismissed the incident in the log: 'Starboard engine has quit shimmying'. He attempted to make light of it by passing a cartoon into the rear cabin of Lyon's eyes bulging out of his head, but as he later acknowledged it had been a genuinely anxious moment. For the rest of the journey all ears strained to hear the slightest irregularity in the engines' unified drone.

Flying through the storms rather than climbing above them paid dividends. Throughout the afternoon Lyon continued to chart impressive progress. By 4.25 pm they were 1,889 kilometres from Kauai, having made an average speed of 171 kilometres per hour. If they could keep the tail wind, prospects of reaching Suva improved markedly. At 5 pm, the heavy storm cells dissipated, leaving a dull haze, thickened by the gathering dusk. Despite being wet, exhausted and with no prospect of a cigarette for at least another 24 hours, Ulm ventured an optimistic forecast in the log: 'Very hazy, but still looks like clearing up for the night'.

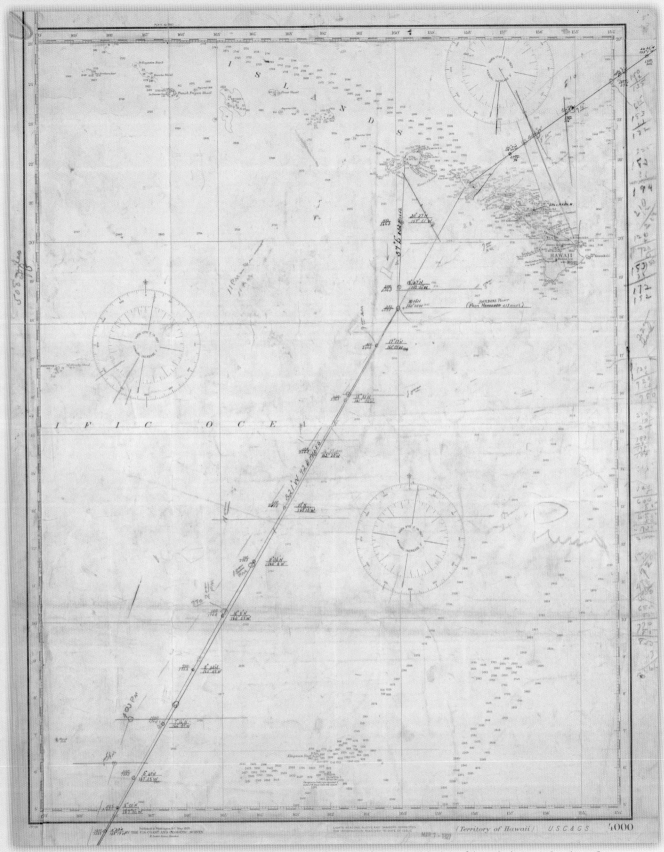

Lyon's charts show that, despite the storms encountered on the afternoon of 3 June and the loss of the radio beacon, Southern Cross made excellent progress and stayed on course.

'A ROTTEN NIGHT AHEAD'

Crossing the equator, 3–5 June 1928

6.30   Hell this rain is rotten. Reminds us
of 2500 mile of rain we flew thro' on
our 7500 mile flt ard Australia
The windshields are leaking & Smithy
and I are getting damned wet too
alt 3500 air speed 69K still climbing

6.50   at 5000 feet we got above rain but had
to swing at right angle to course to do
so. Still higher clouds in front of
us think 6000 feet will see us above
most of them tho' / alt now 5100
Revs. 1700 air speed 65K. climbing /

7.03   for last 10 mins have been flying in circles
to gain altitude to pass over the high
Clouds surrounding us. Heavy rain
intermittently. alt now 6500

7.05   Tis now a race between the clouds
and the Southern Cross as to who shall
reach 10000 feet first. Smithy and
I see a rotten night ahead /

7.15   Now at 7500 feet still battling our way upward
and it's slow going with this Heavy Load

7.31   Sighted the good old Southern Cross
Above our Port Bow. Moon
up also / alt 8,000. above
impenetrable clouds /

96

6.30	Hell this rain is rotten. Reminds us of 2500 miles of rain we flew thru on our 7500 mile flt ard Australia. The windshields are leaking and Smithy and I are getting damned wet too. Alt 3500 Air speed 69K still climbing
6.50	At 5000 feet we got above rain but had to swing at right angle to course to do so. Still higher clouds in front of us Think 6000 feet will see us above most of them tho. Alt now 5100 Revs 1700 airspeed 65K. Climbing.
7.03	For last 15 mins have been flying in circles to gain altitude to pass over high clouds surrounding us. Heavy rain intermittently. Alt now 6500.
7.05	Tis now a race between the clouds and the Southern Cross as to who shall reach 10000 feet first. Smithy and I see a rotten night ahead.
7.15	Now at 7500 feet still battling our way upward and its slow going with this Heavy load.
731	Sighted the good old Southern Cross above our Port Bow. Moon up also. Alt 8000. Above impenetrable clouds.

7.50/   We probably lost an hours flying
in those darker clouds but we
are out of them now and
gliding down to warmer climes.

8.00   Stars are popping out all over
the Heavens. But our group of
Heavenly bodies the S.C. looks best
to us.

11.32   after each other have both had a
refreshing doze — one doesent really
sleep when off duty on a job like this.
but even 10 mins shut eye is helpful

11.33   Lyon reports we have just crossed
the line (equator). Well we are
in our own Hemisphere again.
Instrument dash light failed. Using
hand torch. Height 1800 — Speed
74 K. Revs. 1590. Misty ahead — good
moon and stars. all ok./

12:00 (11:10 Ships Time) Should be over Pheonix Group
but see no sign of them. Lyon sets
new course direct for suva.

4.55   I flew for an hour and half and
been dozing since — well give
Smithy a spell now. Hello
more rain and fluffy clouds
Alt 1300 Av spd. 77 K. Revs 1600

7.50	We probably lost an hours flying in those darned clouds but we are out of them now and gliding down to warmer climes.
8.00	Stars are popping out all over the Heavens. But our group of Heavenly bodies the SC looks best to us.
11.32	after each other have both had a refreshing doze—one doesn't really sleep when off duty on a job like this but even 10 mins shut eye is helpful
11.33	Lyon reports we have just crossed the line (equator). Well we are in our own Hemisphere again. Instrument dash light failed. Using hand torch. Height 1800 – av Speed 74k. Revs 1590. Misty ahead. good moon and stars. All OK.
12.00	(11.10 ships time) Should be over Phoenix Group but see no sign of them. Lyon sets new course direct for Suva.
4.55	Flew for an hour and half and been dozing since—Will give Smithy a spell now. Hello more rain and plenty clouds. alt 1300 airspeed 77 k Revs 1600

Ernest Crome's painting of Southern Cross evokes the miserable conditions the crew endured during the flight from Hawaii to Fiji.

Ulm's optimistic prediction regarding the weather barely lasted the hour. At 6.10 pm, 'thick, heavy cloud banks' began gathering above *Southern Cross*. Estimating the clouds would not extend above 5,000 feet, Kingsford Smith opened the throttles up and began to climb. Still weighed down with a heavy fuel load, the aircraft could only manage about 250 feet per minute. It was going to be a long climb up from 600 feet.

Within five minutes they were among the storm-clouds. Kingsford Smith deviated from their course first one way and then the other, attempting to dodge them. It confounded Lyon's navigation. Wind gusts buffeted the aircraft, rippling its fabric covering and tearing away an exhaust pipe from the centre engine. 'No damage. No Worry', logged Ulm. Beyond the blur of the centre propeller, Kingsford Smith and Ulm could see nothing.

This type of 'blind' flying is exactly what Kingsford Smith had practised with Lieutenant George Pond over Seattle. It involved relying on instruments only in the absence of all exterior visual cues such as the ground or horizon. Kingsford Smith later likened it to being blind and deaf at the same time, with the senses providing none of their normal points of reference to one's orientation. Ulm reckoned it the ultimate test of a pilot's faith in his gauges, 'a contest between your senses and your instruments'.

At 2,000 feet they cleared the storm ceiling, only to find themselves caught in another deluge from thunderstorms above. Shielding his log from the water leaking in around the windshields, Ulm described the scene, noting the 'gorgeous' effect of the setting sun on the ominous blue-black clouds, but quickly adding, 'Hell this rain is rotten'. It reminded him of the 2,000 kilometres of foul weather encountered between Broome and Perth on the flight around Australia the year before. They kept climbing, Kingsford Smith turning at right angles to their course to avoid cloudbursts. In the back, Lyon and Warner had no idea what was going on. The turbulence tossed them about the rear cabin, which had no lighting following the generator's earlier failure. An ink pot tipped, spilling on Lyon's charts, and desperate-sounding appeals appeared in the cockpit from the navigator, who quickly lost track of where they were heading. 'Where the hell are you going—are you turning back?' he asked. 'What the hell are you doing now?' demanded another.

After nearly 40 minutes *Southern Cross* cleared the storm at 5,000 feet. Yet another wall of 'tropical violence' lay ahead, extending up, Ulm reckoned another thousand feet. It appeared threatening enough for Kingsford Smith to momentarily disregard fuel economy and attempt to climb in circles to get above it. Struggling against the turbulence to work his set, Warner provided listeners on both sides of the Pacific with intermittent glimpses of the turmoil through which they were flying. 'It is a race between us and the clouds to the 10,000 feet elevation', he transmitted. 'It is going to be a bad night. The motors are doing heavy pulling now to the 6,500 feet altitude. It is getting dark.'

In Sydney, radio station 2BL's chief engineer Ray Allsop had set up a powerful receiver at his home in Roseville to receive *Southern Cross'* transmissions. Throughout the night, he relayed these to the station, which broadcast them live into the sitting rooms of families around the region. As Warner's faint dots and dashes arrived, Allsop provided a running translation. 'Therefore', as *The Sun* explained to its incredulous readers the following day, 'radio fans actually heard the *Southern Cross'*.

After an hour of climbing, listeners in Sydney learned that the aircraft had finally topped the storm at 7,500 feet and emerged under a clear, star-filled sky. 'There's our friend the moon peeping over a bank of clouds', tapped Warner with his brass key. He sent personal greetings to a number of friends ('Jim's thinking of you all') followed by a reassuring sign-off to conserve the batteries: 'Sure having a nice ride here among the clouds. We now a bit away from the clouds but a solid heavy rolling mass under us'.

Levelling out at 8,000 feet, Ulm described the stars 'popping out all over the Heavens' in the log. Among them, the Southern Cross appeared, heralding his and Kingsford Smith's imminent return to their own hemisphere after almost a year. As they left the storm behind, Kingsford Smith descended to less frigid altitudes and the crew settled back into the routine of night flying.

At 11.30 pm, with the weather still calm, a jab in the back woke Ulm. A message from Lyon appeared, stating they had just crossed the equator and that they should soon be over the Phoenix islands. As well as representing a haven for emergency landing, in the absence of the radio beacon and ships, the islands would provide Lyon with the only opportunity on this leg to confirm his dead reckoning. For half an hour all eyes aboard *Southern Cross* eagerly searched for them, shadows cast by the moonlight producing several false sightings. Just before midnight, Lyon sent a message forward presenting the flight's co-commanders with a difficult decision. They should, he estimated, be right over the Phoenix islands. If they continued on their present southerly course they would cut across the Samoan islands, about 880 kilometres away. Alternatively Lyon suggested, they could steer a course to Suva, which lay an estimated 2,000 kilometres to the south-west.

It all came down to fuel. After a tense discussion on note paper, Ulm and Kingsford Smith agreed that they had enough left to make it to Fiji if the wind cooperated and they had no more bad weather to avoid. Of critical importance was the accuracy of Lyon's dead reckoning. Without sighting the Phoenix islands he could not be entirely sure

For an aircraft of its size, Southern Cross *had relatively small control surfaces, making it difficult to handle, especially in bad weather. Its broad wing and large, fixed undercarriage didn't help either.*

of where they were, making the decision to continue to Fiji a real gamble. Unknown to any of the crew, however, at that moment the crew of the *Sonoma*, a ship en route to Australia from San Francisco, heard *Southern Cross* pass overhead. They were among the Phoenix islands, something they tried to communicate to Warner but that he could not receive owing to the dead receiver battery. On instructions from the cockpit, Lyon dialled up a new heading on the Earth Inductor Compass, steering them for Suva.

Just before dawn, the heavy, languid calm came to an end, replaced again by lashing rain and wind gusts that caused *Southern Cross* to pitch and heave violently. Ahead, an enormous black nimbus cloud, lit up by flashes of blue lightning, loomed up some 12,000 feet. 'Smithy looked worried and worn out', recalled Ulm. Knowing they could not possibly get above such a towering storm, Kingsford Smith instructed Warner to reel in the antennae and descended to 400 feet in an attempt to pass beneath it. Torrents of rain and violent air currents threw

Southern Cross' open-sided cockpit made speaking impossible, fur-lined overalls necessary and often resulted in the pilots being drenched by rain.

the aircraft about violently, making it dangerous to be so low and compelling Kingsford Smith to change his mind and climb into the storm. The instrument panel light had blown, so Ulm held a torch on the gauges.

After an hour, they were back at 8,000 feet. The sun was just coming up, revealing as Ulm wrote in the log, 'a cheerless dawn—rain, cold and blind flying'. The climbing and dodging about worried both pilots. Kingsford Smith was convinced that they were 'out of luck', and would be forced to ditch in the ocean before sighting land. To Lyon, he wrote an uncharacteristically anxious-sounding note. 'Harry can't you get a star position at all? Or can't Jim get a radio bearing? Getting pretty serious if we don't get one in a few hours.' Ulm remained slightly more optimistic about the fuel but he doubted they were still on course after all the erratic manoeuvring.

To conserve fuel, Kingsford Smith took them back down to 500 feet. They met with more bad luck, though; the prevailing north-easterly tail winds enjoyed the previous afternoon had been replaced by a vigorous south-westerly headwind. It sapped Ulm's optimism and brought the rest of the crew's spirits down to rock bottom. Notes from Warner and Lyon appeared asking about the fuel situation. Kingsford Smith levelled with them: 'We have 5 hours gas and are only making about 60 knots [111 kilometres per hour] against wind'. Lyon's last sextant shot had put them 1,277 kilometres from Suva. It was not encouraging arithmetic; as Warner explained in his characteristically wry fashion, it 'left about 170 miles to swim and me with a bad corn on each foot'. He wasn't alone. Even Ulm acknowledged in the log at 9.30 am that it was 'doubtful' they would reach Suva, though he still held out hope for reaching land.

A sudden change in the bleak outlook came just after 10 am. Ulm, trying the hand-pump instead of the motorised pump, shifted the last fuel from the auxiliary into the main tanks and discovered that more remained than they had calculated. It was enough, in fact, to keep them airborne for an additional two hours beyond their previous predictions. 'Whoops of joy on board', he recorded. 'We'll make it now OK. Hot dam.'

Around midday, after another six hours of tropical thunderstorms, the weather finally cleared, leaving a dull overcast day. Ulm logged that they had been in the air for 32 hours and should be sighting land soon. The crew began what Warner described as the 'grim game' of watching the horizon for land. 'If no member of the team sights land before the gas gives out your side loses and you don't need an umpire.'

For an hour and a half they flew on, bucking against the headwind. Warner kept transmitting their position, but because of the broken generator could not receive bearings from land-based stations. He watched Lyon with mounting anxiety, noting the navigator's 'noble brow corrugated' with worry as he checked and re-checked his dead reckoning.

Unable to hold on any longer, Warner had to relieve himself in the cabin. The crew typically used a bottle when they needed to urinate, afterwards emptying it out the window. At this moment, however, Warner required something more substantial in the way of relief and spread out a newspaper on the floor to squat over. At the most inopportune time, *Southern Cross* hit turbulence, causing the hapless radio operator to fall into his own mess. Already stripped to his underwear and singlet, he was forced to jettison these and complete the flight naked.

At 1.10 pm Ulm sighted the north coast of Vanua Levu, the second largest island of the Fiji group. According to Lyon, 'the excitement and relief was immense'. Ulm recalled that he and Kingsford Smith 'nudged each other in delight … we were on the verge of triumph'. Within two minutes, they could see islands everywhere on the starboard horizon. 'We were soon flying low over some of the sweetest looking little

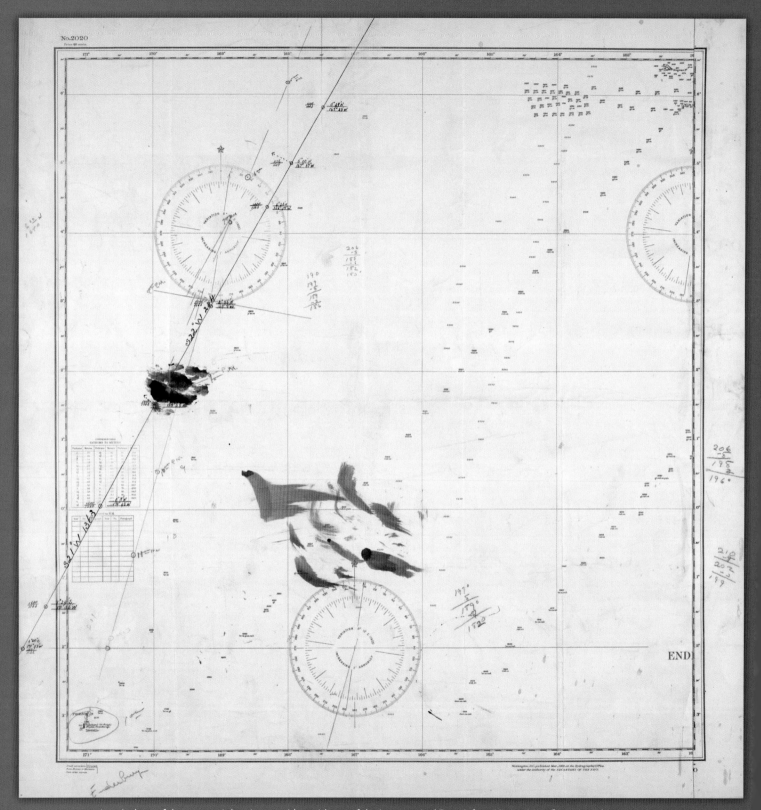

Lyon's chart of the equatorial region provides evidence of the Intertropical Front's fury. His position fixes record variations in Southern Cross' ground speed from 68 to 145 kilometres per hour and the map bears the stains of ink spilled in the turbulence.

islands ever constructed', recalled Warner. 'Even the coral reefs looked good enough to eat.' In the moments that followed, as they swept in low over Fiji's northern islands, Ulm made a triumphant declaration to Kingsford Smith on the back page of the log. 'The rest is easy. Its hard to realize its over and that at the moment we are exceedingly famous.' The events of the previous 30 hours had, however, tempered his confidence that he and Kingsford Smith could do the last leg alone. 'I've nearly changed my views re taking Jim on to Aussie with us. Remind me to talk with you re this' (this is reproduced on page 166).

For an hour and a half *Southern Cross* passed over dozens of islands separated by translucent green water. At 3.45 pm, they circled Suva, their landing ground at Albert Park clearly marked out by the thousands of Fijians surrounding it, with, as one journalist described it, their 'great fuzzy hair' and 'dressed in all colours of the rainbow'. The local government had cleared trees and telegraph poles from the park, but warned that it would not be big enough to handle an aircraft. Nonetheless, everyone on board still expressed shock at how small it looked from the air: 'about as large as a pocket-handkerchief', reckoned Warner, 'and not half as useful'. Almost despairing, Kingsford Smith circled the town

Southern Cross *at Richmond aerodrome, near Sydney, shortly after the Pacific flight in 1928. Finding airstrips long enough to accommodate it proved one of the key logistical challenges of the journey.*

and bay, seeking a better landing spot. Not seeing any, he turned back and ordered the Americans to climb into the tail. Still naked following his toilet misfortune, Warner, along with Lyon in his underwear, clambered through the maze of wires, careful not to put their feet through the aircraft's floor, which in the extreme aft section, consisted of canvas only.

Inspecting Albert Park today, it is obvious that landing a three-engine aircraft without wheel brakes there was a remarkably risky thing. High ground to the park's north, east and south meant that Kingsford Smith had to approach from over the water, from the west. From this direction, however, he had to clear the Grand Pacific Hotel, situated between the bay and the park, and then a road flanking the park's western edge on a 3-metre embankment. The park's diminutive length—330 metres—meant that Kingsford Smith had to touch down as close to the road as possible if he hoped to avoid crashing into the tree line at the park's far end.

He brought *Southern Cross* in over the bay at 100 kilometres per hour, just clearing the hotel roof. As they crossed the road and dropped suddenly, Ulm felt ill, certain they were about to crash. The crowd gasped and the wheels touched down, 45 metres inside the park. The aircraft bounced back into the air and then slammed down again. It sped on towards the trees, Kingsford Smith whipping the aircraft around in a dramatic 180-degree turn at the last

moment. The machine stopped, right between two trees at the end of the park. 'The plane', as one journalist breathlessly reported, 'had nothing whatever to spare'.

Descriptions of the dramatic landing appeared in newspapers all around the world in the following hours. They all emphasise the extreme peril of the landing, how it nearly resulted in a catastrophic accident and the remarkable skill of Kingsford Smith's 'ground loop'. What none of them mentioned, however, and what Ulm neglected to note in the log, was Warner's brush with death. When Kingsford Smith bounced *Southern Cross*, the force sent the radio operator crashing through the tail section's canvas floor. The aircraft trundled on leaving him naked and unconscious in the mud. Fortunately a British nurse rushed forward and, after covering him with her cape, established that miraculously he had escaped injury from the aircraft's tail wheel. The incident remained outside the trans-Pacific flight's narrative for three decades. None of the crew mentioned it in their memoirs and no journalist acknowledged it in the press (*The Sun* reported that 'Warner exited first' after landing, which strictly speaking was not untrue). The story emerged in 1958, told by an elderly Warner to a *Sunday Telegraph* reporter when he visited Australia to mark the flight's 30th anniversary.

'About as large as a pocket handkerchief and not half as useful': Kingsford Smith only narrowly avoided disaster when landing Southern Cross at Albert Park.

'LOOKS CLEAR AHEAD'

Interlude in Fiji, 5–8 June 1928

Took off Suva   2.52 pm
Revs 1810. Airspeed 84 K.
880 galls
                    100 ft 1st minute
flew low back over crowd on beach
2.55 Throttled back to 1750 R Pm

3.04 Passed over town of Suva. cheering population

4.20 Ever since takeoff E1C been out of action
      and we been trying fix same. changing course
      all the while in endeavour & find what's
      wrong. Now flying by Steering compasses on
      235°. but Lyon fears them to be inaccurate
      as small metal objects which would affect
      them have since been placed in Nav. Cabin.
      We don't blame E1C but feel it may
      have been inadvertently damaged at Vaselau
      beach. The E1C is a wonderful compass
      and we miss it greatly.
          Lyon informs me that Aperiodic and
      Steering compass practically agree. That good.
      Revolutions 1675 airspeed 76 K alt. 1500 all
      OK.

4.35 Cloudy above but looks clear ahead.
      I suggested to Lyon that he take bearing
      on land if possible and try and check
      Aperiodic and Steering compasses.
          We tried new method of stopping sun
      lens today. we used plastacine.

Took off Suva 2.52 pm

Revs 1810 airspeed 84 k

880 galls

100 ft 1st minute

Flew low back over crowd on beach

2.55   Throttled back to 1750 RPM

3.04   Passed over town of Suva cheering population

4.20   Ever since take off EIC been out of action and we
been trying fix same. Changing course all the while in
endeavour to find whats wrong. Now flying by steering
compasses on 235°. But Lyon fears them to be unusable
as small metal objects which would affect them have
since been placed in Nav cabin. We don't blame EIC but
feel it may have been inadvertently damaged at Naselai
Beach. The EIC is a wonderful compass, and we miss
it greatly.

Lyon informs me that Aperiodic and Steering compass
practically agree. Thats good. Revolutions 1675 Airspeed
76 K Alt. 1500 All OK.

4.25   Cloudy above but looks clear ahead. I suggested to Lyon
that he take bearing on Sun if possible and try and check
aperiodic and steering compasses.

We tried new method stopping our ears today. We used
plastacine.

'Waving arms and open
mouths, all shouting…
locked us in on every side.'

Southern Cross had left Kauai at 5.22 am on Sunday, 3 June 1928. It covered the 5,000 kilometres to Suva in 34 hours and 30 minutes, but because of the International Date Line, arrived in Fiji in the early afternoon of Tuesday, 5 June. Unlike in Hawaii, Ulm would not record his experiences in Fiji in the log. From other sources, such as the aviators' memoirs and reports from news correspondents, it's clear that the flight's 'organising manager' did not have time to give the log a thought during this stopover. Lacking the assistance of the United States military and with only basic local infrastructure, Ulm would need to bring to bear his utmost skills at coordinating resources and managing people to get *Southern Cross* back into the air for the journey's final leg.

Before the propellers had even stopped spinning, the crowds lining Albert Park's perimeter surged forward and surrounded *Southern Cross*. Pith-helmeted British soldiers, their presence organised in advance by Ulm, cordoned off the aircraft just in time. The crew emerged from the cabin dishevelled, bleary-eyed and, looking according to one reporter, 'grey and nervy'. Ulm recalled how 'waving arms and open mouths, all shouting something at us, locked us in on every side'. When a journalist called to him, asking if they intended to head for Brisbane tomorrow, he snapped, 'Give us a chance. We do not know yet'. Moments later, a car conveying the Mayor and Governor parted the crowd and arrived to rescue the aviators from the barrage

By radio, Ulm instructed Suva's authorities to provide necessary measures for keeping crowds a safe distance from the aeroplane.

of questions, photographs and autograph-hunters. Ulm shook the Governor's hand and inhaled deeply on a cigarette. 'Phew! That's better. That's just what I wanted.' Kingsford Smith, 'stone deaf', kept asking people to repeat themselves, while Lyon continuously apologised for his scruffy appearance.

Satisfied with the ring of soldiers and native police surrounding *Southern Cross*, the airmen were driven across the crowded park to the Grand Pacific Hotel, where the Mayor had offered to host them. They joined the official party on the hotel's balcony, overlooking the park. To an audience of some 10,000 locals, for whom the day had been proclaimed a public holiday, the Mayor gave a speech that, as one reporter explained, 'stammered with an emotion shared by all'. Kingsford Smith replied; his typical swagger noticeably absent. He admitted

it had been a harrowing night and put their safe arrival down to the skill of his American colleagues. Lyon then spoke, directing credit back to Kingsford Smith's flying and toasting with a high ball of whisky. 'We would willingly do the trip again for stuff like that.'

Over a meal, Kingsford Smith and Ulm made plans for the next leg. Ulm hoped to fly to Brisbane the following day, but both agreed that it would be impossible to take off from Albert Park fully loaded. They would need to find and prepare an alternative airstrip from which to start the journey's final stage. Local pilots reckoned they might not get away for four or five days, something Ulm considered 'a matter of grave concern'. Ulm and Kingsford Smith also probably discussed taking the Americans, or at least Warner, on to Brisbane. As their contract stood they would otherwise

The Mayor of Suva and a Fijian chief greet the Pacific fliers.

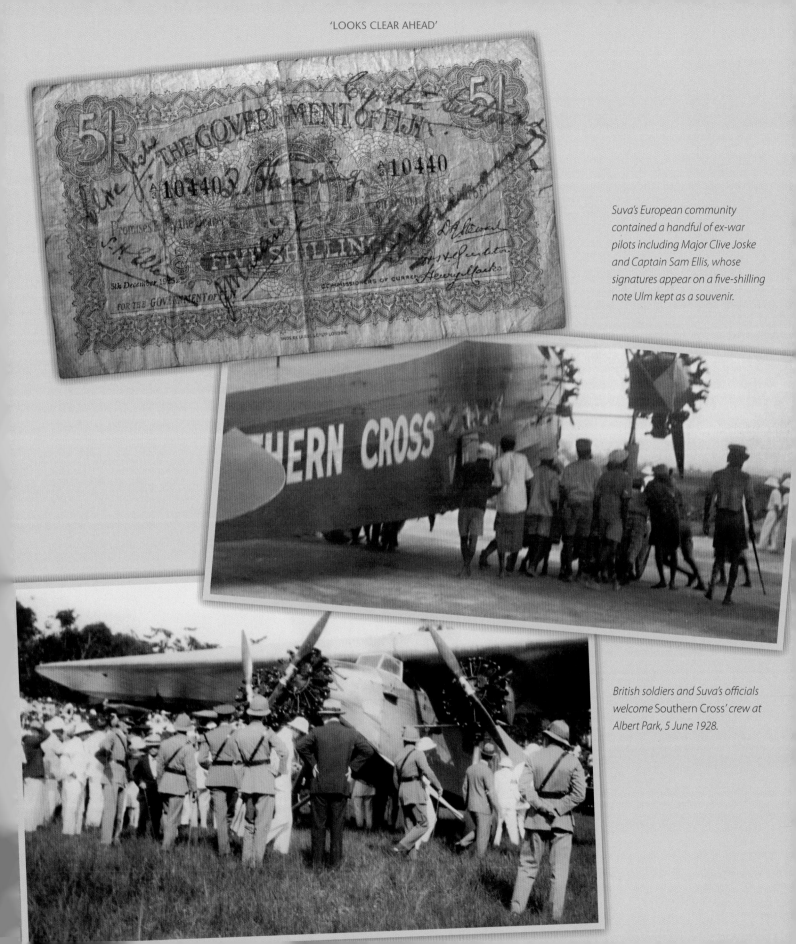

Suva's European community contained a handful of ex-war pilots including Major Clive Joske and Captain Sam Ellis, whose signatures appear on a five-shilling note Ulm kept as a souvenir.

British soldiers and Suva's officials welcome Southern Cross' crew at Albert Park, 5 June 1928.

be boarding an ocean liner for the United States in two days' time, leaving the two Australians to fly to Brisbane by themselves.

Ulm and Kingsford Smith hit the ground running the following morning. After a breakfast of kippers, bacon and eggs, and some quick photographs with hotel guests and reporters in the lobby ('I feel like a million dollars', Ulm told one), the two airmen split up to inspect possible take-off sites. As in Hawaii, the cooperation of local authorities proved crucial. The Governor loaned Kingsford Smith his private boat to sail out to Naselai beach, the most distant option at 30 kilometres away. He would be gone most of the day. The manager of Colonial Sugar Refining meanwhile

escorted Ulm to nearby Nausori, inland from Suva, where he inspected two sites but found that the most suitable would require 300 men and 24 hours to prepare. Whichever location they selected, getting *Southern Cross* there, along with fuel in time to take off the following day, represented an immense logistical challenge.

Finding a solution to this problem should have occupied the rest of Ulm's day, but commitments to the press and Suva's social scene intervened in a most frustrating manner. Returning to Suva, he cabled his log entries from the previous leg to *The Sun*—some 2,000 words that would appear in the following afternoon's edition. He then tended to the dozens of cables pouring in

Suva's central business district as it appeared around the time of the trans-Pacific flight.

from around the world, from everyone, it seems, from the Australian Prime Minister to the Limbless Soldiers' Conference, meeting in Sydney that day. Most offered congratulations but some related matters requiring Ulm's immediate attention. Plans for their arrival at Eagle Farm aerodrome in Brisbane and the subsequent publicity tour to Sydney, Melbourne and Canberra consumed his morning. With characteristic thoroughness he cabled instructions covering every detail: from where spectators should be arranged to how many police were required and where they needed to stand to maintain a safe boundary around the aircraft.

Meanwhile, around the world, the four Pacific fliers had made an overnight transition from relative obscurity to household names. Their personal lives and pasts suddenly became fair game for the pressmen. *The LA Examiner*, for example, tracked down the estranged wives of Warner and Lyon, both of whom professed hopes for reconciliation with their now-famous husbands. The interest in the fliers' personal lives, augmented by the press' insatiable appetite for a 'scoop', spread the limelight from Kingsford Smith to the party's other members. Ulm even received this fitting tribute from Hobart's *Mercury*, in a story on the 'trying ordeal' of his wife Jo, whom he had married a fortnight before leaving Australia and had not seen in almost a year.

'Give us a chance. We do not know yet': The nervous tension of the previous night is written all over Ulm's face as he and Kingsford Smith battle through the crowd at Albert Park.

Mrs Ulm absolutely radiates confidence, pointing to the optimistic tone of all the letters she has received, and also to the fact that never before was an endurance flight embarked on with such wonderful organising. The work is very largely due to Ulm, whose energy and devotion to detail are amazing.

Ulm and the Americans spent the rest of the day being whisked from one reception to another. After lunch with the Governor, they attended a civic event in Suva's town hall where the townsfolk showered them with gifts. From Fiji's oldest chief, Ulm accepted a whale's tooth, a traditional symbol of best wishes, and from Suva's schoolchildren, Lyon and Warner received an American flag made of flowers. The ex-servicemen of Suva hosted the airmen for afternoon tea at a luxurious villa in the 'picturesque heights' of Tamavua, overlooking the town and bay. Ulm later admitted that all this lavish hospitality was lost on him. He was weary and anxious to press on with the journey's final stage.

That evening the fliers attended a ball at the Pacific Grand Hotel, joined by Suva's 'youth and beauty'. They proved a hit with the local girls who badgered them for dances all night. The Americans, sporting new blue dinner suits, obliged but Ulm, wearing the riding boots, shirt and breeches he had left Oakland in, spent most of the night attending to business. During dinner Kingsford Smith returned from his day-long reconnaissance to report that he had found a suitable runway on Naselai beach. To the soundtrack of foxtrots and waltzes, Ulm

made hurried arrangements with the Mayor and his staff to have fuel and supplies shipped to Naselai. Before the final dance, work gangs at the harbour were loading stocks of timber, fuel, oil and tools onto the government's boat *Pioneer*, ready to sail the following morning.

The evening ended with the presentation to the fliers of a turtle shell chest containing 200 gold sovereigns. They were seen out of the ballroom by a line of young ladies, most of whom were content with a handshake, although a few stole a kiss. Warner described the ball 'an affair worth remembering', and recalled how Lyon finished asleep on the Governor's shoulder, something Sir Eyre Hutson 'bore with becoming modesty'.

The following day, *The Sun* published a cable from Kingsford Smith (though it almost certainly came from Ulm) announcing that despite their engagement officially ending in Fiji, the Americans had been invited to fly to Brisbane 'where they will finally leave the expedition'. The cable claimed that the Australians had done this out of their 'sincere appreciation' and as 'a sportsmanlike act'.

What the cable, which newspapers around Australia and the United States quickly reproduced, did not reveal, however, was that Ulm and Kingsford Smith had more pragmatic motives. We know from a scribbled note at the back of the log that during the flight from Kauai to Suva Ulm had started having second thoughts about taking Warner on to Brisbane. The dangerous tropical weather had evidently

Despite the Americans' dissatisfaction with their contracts, the Pacific fliers managed to maintain a united front for the cameras.

demonstrated the value of having a wireless operator, who could assist with radio navigation and call for help in an emergency, not to mention supply the press with exciting progress updates that would fuel public interest in the expedition. We also know from another note in the back of the log during the Hawaii–Fiji leg that Ulm had lost some confidence in Lyon. In a scribbled conversation with Kingsford Smith, Ulm expressed concern 'that Harry had beggered up the long[itude]' using the artificial horizon on his sextant. He went to visit his Navy friends at Pearl Harbor to have it calibrated, but Ulm believed Lyon had instead 'got drunk' with them.

After arriving in Suva, another force came to bear on the decision when Ulm and Kingsford Smith began receiving telegrams urging them to bring the Americans to Australia. Newspapers were beginning to question the fairness of leaving them in Fiji and the Australian public had developed quite a curiosity in the expedition's 'invisible' members, especially Warner, whose staccato dots and dashes had held them glued to their wireless sets. Kingsford Smith's father allegedly cabled a warning to his son not to bother coming to Australia if he left the Americans behind.

The issue came up back in the hotel suite following the ball. Everyone was weary, at the end of a boozy afternoon and evening, and probably not in their best form. Ulm, it appears, remained opposed to Lyon completing the air journey to Australia, but suggested as a compromise that he follow *Southern Cross* to Brisbane by sea. Losing his temper, Lyon slammed Ulm up against the hotel wall and was about to start with his fists when Kingsford Smith stepped in and convinced Ulm to change his mind.

The following morning Ulm employed a local solicitor to draw up new contracts for the Americans, offering them an additional £100 (approximately $7,000 today) each 'as an act of grace' to continue with *Southern Cross* to Brisbane 'but not further'. Warner and Lyon signed, but resented what they perceived as Ulm's unnecessarily bureaucratic approach and avaricious spirit. Ulm saw things more pragmatically. The contract described him and Kingsford Smith as the flight's 'owners' and noted that they had 'incurred a personal liability of upwards of US$50,000' in organising it. Ulm considered the Americans employees being paid a generous wage for a finite period. The contract carefully specified they had no claim to any further share of wealth that the flight should generate.

Ulm and Kingsford Smith, with *The Sun*'s help, managed to keep the whole fractious incident out of the Australian press. Presenting a scoop on the new plans the following day, *The Sun* claimed rather opaquely that

after breakfast a hurried conference of the two Australians resulted in gladdening the Americans' hearts as in truly sportsmanlike manner they offered them a passage to Australia, despite the fact that their contracts finished at Suva, and that their presence was unnecessary for the next span.

Warner, who bore out the incident with a cynical passivity, would later attempt to set the record straight by publishing the entire contents of the contract in an account of the flight he wrote for American magazine *Liberty*, in April 1930. 'Isn't it cute', he concluded sardonically. 'Yes, we signed it. You know the saying. "When in Rome, act like a Roman candle!" Well, when in the company of sportsmen, reward true munificence by a like gesture; in other words, act like a true sport.'

Delayed at Naselai, 7 June

The following morning, Kingsford Smith flew *Southern Cross* from Albert Park to Naselai. To get off the ground with such a short run, he took minimum fuel and left Ulm and the Americans behind to make the journey by sea. Even with the barest load, *Southern Cross* cleared the park's western embankment by only 6 metres. Thousands had gathered and they cheered as Kingsford Smith circled, waved and

Unanticipated delays: refuelling Southern Cross *at Naselai beach, 7 June 1928.*

then set out over the bay. The people of Suva then went to work, something one journalist reckoned they had not done since *Southern Cross'* arrival two days before.

Arriving at Naselai in mid-afternoon, it pleased Ulm to find things on schedule. Fijians, with 'gleaming bronze bodies', ferried drums of fuel from *Pioneer* onto the beach, riding the breakers in their canoes, Ulm observed, 'with the same certainty as the club boats on Sydney's beaches'. Throughout the afternoon, the crew made preparations to take off before sunset. Watching the activity around *Southern Cross* that afternoon, a correspondent for *The Sun* made a neat pen-sketch of the four very different characters who comprised its crew.

Ulm was already busy supervising every detail, his clean white shirt already oil stained. He was strung at high tension. Kingsford Smith, the imperturbable, was in the navigator's cabin aft reading the local press reports and finding the press accounts more wonderful than the flight itself. With Lyon still full of beans and jovial and Warner, still immaculate, they form a happy brotherly band of gallant, modest men.

Ulm and Kingsford Smith had decided they only needed 3,406 litres (about three-quarters capacity) of fuel for this, the journey's shortest leg. Nonetheless, man-handling the fuel ashore through heavy surf and up the beach to *Southern Cross* where it had to be filtered into the tanks through a chamois, took more time than Ulm had allowed. By his nominated take-off time of 4 pm it was obvious, to his immense irritation, that they were not going to get away before

'Busy supervising every detail': Ulm makes final checks before embarking on the journey's last stretch, Naselai beach, 8 June 1928.

the tide again swallowed up much of the makeshift airstrip. Dejected, Ulm arranged for the labourers to haul *Southern Cross* up to the tree line and cover the engines for the night. Delaying take-off until the following (Friday) morning sounded the death knell to Ulm's chances of eating in Sydney on Saturday night.

Kingsford Smith, Ulm and Lyon spent the night offshore on *Pioneer*, enjoying the hospitality, including steaks, pineapples and cold beers, of its captain. Warner remained on the beach with a British police sergeant and his party of native constabulary to watch the aircraft. 'My election to this post of honour was practically unanimous', observed Warner wryly. 'I won by a majority of something like seventy five per cent.'

In the event, the evening provided Warner with a truly unique experience, one that would stand out in his mind as a highlight of the whole journey. Assured that *Southern Cross* was in safe hands with the police, the sergeant led Warner and a newspaper correspondent to a Fijian village, a few kilometres back from the beach. The chief hosted Warner in his home, at what the American described as a 'gab fest' among the village elders. With the police sergeant interpreting, Warner regaled them with the story of his journey across 'the big water'. It left his audience bewildered; they attributed the humble American wireless operator, who a few weeks before had been a door-to-door salesman, with supernatural powers. 'It was a humorous night', reported the journalist,

Fijians provided the Pacific fliers with crucial assistance in preparing Southern Cross *for take-off at Naselai.*

'One of the most charming little ceremonies I have ever witnessed': Southern Cross' crew partake in the kava ceremony before taking off.

'watching the interpreter endeavouring to explain to the bewildered natives the mysteries of radio'. The elders honoured Warner with a kava ceremony and a traditional singing and dancing performance. Following several coconut shells of the brew ('It looks like mud and tastes like Gregory powder') Warner, concerned about its potency, asked to return to the aircraft.

Returning to the beach a couple of kilometres from the aircraft, Warner and the police sergeant were horrified to see a huge fire. 'It looked as though the *Southern Cross* was blazing merrily and we broke into a run, expecting any moment to hear the explosion that would mark the end of the first plane to cross the Pacific.' Covering the distance 'in nothing flat', Warner discovered that the native police had built a huge bonfire 'entirely too near' the aircraft: it was showering sparks all over the blue fabric fuselage. Heaping sand onto the fire, they averted potential disaster. Warner retired to the aircraft's cabin while the police sergeant berated his men. 'He was so aroused that he dropped into English at times and I gathered that he was bringing up intimate details in the family life of the immediate ancestors of each man.' Warner spent a chilled night on the timber floorboards, 'a can for a pillow'.

The following morning, Warner woke to find *Southern Cross*' nose 'nestling in the tropical scrub above the high water mark, and the sea lazily lapping her tail'. The tide would not expose enough of the beach for *Southern Cross* to take off until mid-afternoon. As it receded, the Fijian helpers manhandled the aircraft into position. A little after 2 pm, as the crew made ready to leave, the villagers appeared, led by a procession of girls in grass skirts bearing kava. Kingsford Smith recalled being 'deeply touched by one of the most charming little ceremonies I have ever witnessed'.

Southern Cross took off at 2.52 pm after a run of about 900 metres. Flying a much lighter plane than previously, Kingsford Smith could whip the aircraft back around and roar in low over the beach, and then across to Suva where the streets and Albert Park had once again filled with cheering locals, wishing them well for the journey's final stretch.

'WORST 2½ HOURS ON WHOLE FLIGHT'

Pacific storm, 8–9 June 1928

5:00 Position. Lat 19°28'S Long 175°34'E
180 nautical miles from Suva
Auge 89½ knots per hour

5:45 Sunset - Port Radio Generator running
again O.K. - Still looks like clear
night ahead - One compass still
dis out of order - Speed 70K climbing
Alt 3850 Revs 1650! getting quite
colder

6:15 Again the Exhaust pipes are
Spitting fire - Darkness has set in -
Smith + I both now crawl into our
fur lined overalls. It's quite
Cold now. Altitude 4300
Airspeed 70K climbing Revs 1650
One compass Still out. This is
the best night so far and we
are making good time but
we will strike headwinds after
passing New Caledonia

11:07 Since last entry have passed
through worst 2½ hours on whole
flight. Terrific Rain storms with
Very violent bumps sometimes
losing 400ft in one bump

5.00   Position. Lat 19° 25S Long 175° 34E

180 nautical miles from Suva

Avge 89½ knots per hour

5.45   Sunset—Port Radio Generator running again OK. Still looks like clear night ahead—one compass still out of order—speed 70k climbing alt 3850 Revs 1650. getting ~~quite~~ colder

6.15   Again the exhaust pipes are spitting fire. Darkess has set in.

Smithy & I both now crawl into our fur lined overalls. Its quite cold now. Altitude 4300 airspeed 70 K climbing Revs 1650. One compass still out. This is the best night so far and we are making good time but we will strike headwinds after passing New Caledonia.

11.07   Since last entry have passed through worst 2½ hours on whole flight. Terrific rainstorm with very violent bumps sometimes losing 400 ft in one bump

and incessant rain. We rose to 7800
feet but could not get above
it Still very wet, It was
a case of fly thro' it and plane
very difficult to control, At times
when I flying blind the bumps
were so bad as to necessitate all
the strength of both of us on the
wheel +. Have been 8 hours in
air and Smithy flown 5½ and
self 2½. Will relieve him
again now / Alt now 4400
AirSpeed 70K and just
encountering more bumps
which indicate another storm

3.70AM For past 4 hours have been
dodging up and down at alts
between 500 and 9000 feet
at present at 1500 having

132

and incessant rain. We rose to 7800 feet but could not get above it S + U got very wet. It was a case of fly thro' it and plane very difficult to control. At times when S flying blind the bumps were so bad as to necessitate all the strength of both of us on the wheel. Have been 8 hours in air and Smithy flown 5½ and self 2½. Will relieve him again now. Alt now 4400 Airspeed 70 K and just encountering more bumps which indicate another storm.

3.20am For past 4 hours have been dodging up and down at alts between 500 and 9000 feet at present at 1500 having [just left several nasty rainstorms but none of them compared to the first one.]

EXTRA

NET SALES LARGER THAN THOSE OF ANY OTHER NEWSPAPER IN AUSTRALIA

THE ☀ SUN

ABOVE ALL

"FOR AUSTRALIA"

No. 5486 (Registered at the General Post Office, Sydney, for transmission by post as a newspaper.) SYDNEY : FRIDAY, JUNE 8, 1928 'Phones: B6021 to B6029

"We Are in Air Again, Bound for Aussie"

LIKE HAWK!

SOUTHERN CROSS HOP-OFF

SUVA WATCHES

WHERE PRAWNS ARE RED

(By "The Sun's" Special Representative)

SUVA, Friday.

From Tamavua village four miles out from Suva, one dominates the town. The point overlooks the flat delta of Rewa to the east to Naselai, 0 miles away. To-day, in an atmosphere of clear skies with the seas showing their brightest blues, merging into turquoise over the coral reef which ringed the surf, it was just possible to discern the Pioneer, gleaming white, anchored in the lagoon at Naselai.

Courteous Gesture

Fijians for miles around are busy engaged removing every particle of seaweed, driftwood, and rocks from the beach until it is clean and smooth enough to satisfy any housewife. Gradually the tide recedes, sufficiently to give a good taking-off space. The engines start. Ulm, Lyon and Warner clamber in. The throttle is opened, the engines roar and shut out the world. The machine waddles forward, the speed increases, the tail lifts and she's off like a sparrowhawk circling and diving in the middle distance.

So like a bigger bird is it that the main shape seen moving over the palms is at first mistaken for a hawk, when a loud cry brings the whole village swarming about us. The Aorangi about opposite the beach at the ... to-off. The machine is ... sighted ...

TO VICTORY

"ENGINE PURRING BEAUTIFULLY"

To Beating Heart of Brisbane

STORY FROM 'PLANE

From Silver Sands of Suva

EVERYTHING O.K.; EXPECT TO LAND IN 18 HOURS

(By Captain Kingsford Smith and C. T. P. Ulm)

ABOARD THE SOUTHERN CROSS, Friday.

The Southern Cross took off from the Naselai Beach, 20 miles from Suva, on the last hop to Brisbane at 3 p.m. (1 p.m. Sydney time). We flew over Suva, the engines purring beautifully.

Well, here we are on the way again! Everything is O.K. In 19 or 20 hours we will be in dear old Aussie again. Landing at Brisbane will be the culmination of 10 months' hard work and the realisation of our ambition to be the first to really cross the Pacific by air. After arriving in Brisbane, we will leave the next day for Sydney. We can assure the Brisbane public that we will return after a couple of weeks rest. Cheerio.

2.30 p.m. (Sydney time): Please convey to Mayor Marks, of Suva, and all the residents our truly sincere and grateful appreciation of all that has been done for us.

2.54 p.m.: Ever since we left Sydney nearly eleven months ago we have felt sure that no matter how black the prospects were at the time, we would be able to ... fly the Pacific, and here we are ...

self-appointed task. We had a long, but narrow strip of beach to take off from Naselai, with a fairly strong cross-wind, but comparatively speaking only a light load on board—880 gallons of petrol and 32 gallons of oil.

Ahead it looks as if it will be our first clear night since the start of the flight. Till Brisbane we will be there about ...

who, then, in the most unselfish manner, saw us through, details of which cannot be given here. But we take the opportunity of publicly thanking him for the most modern manner—that is by radio, from the first aeroplane crossing the Pacific Ocean.

We are not, of course, forgetting our many friends who have helped us. We will soon be able to thank them personally, particularly Mr. Sid-

possibility of dirty weather to-night. Hence Ulm will relieve Smithy at the control now, so that he may better be rested for the night flying. We are as happy as Larry up here. Coo-ee.

SUVA, Friday.

After a nice take-off from the Recreation Ground at Suva, and after waiting for an hour and a half in the air until the tide receded, we landed at

CLOUDS FORECAST

BETTER NEAR BRISBANE

BRISBANE, Friday.

The Commonwealth Meteorologist transmitted the following special forecast to the Southern Cross fliers at 10 o'clock to-day:

Fresh east to E.N.E. breeze and broken clouds to about 170 degrees east where wind changing to south-east, with increasing cloud and some showers. Clouds breaking beyond 165 degrees east, and weather improving towards the mainland with south-easterly winds. Course south of direct route equally safe and slight advantage due to wind direction.

MYSTERIES

RADIO AND KAVA

WARNER'S NIGHT OUT

ON THE NASELAI BEACH

("Sun" Special)

SUVA, Friday.

Warner's night on the beach at Naselai was preceded by a round of revelry, during which kava was handed out.

Kava, as every tourist knows, is a ceremonial drink of the South Seas. It looks like mud, and tastes like Gregory powder. Warner, as guest of honor, had to drink deep often, and spin a tale or two.

It was a humorous sight watching the interpreter endeavoring to explain to the bewildered natives the mysteries of radio.

rendered valuable organising assistance.

The Governor (Sir Eyre Hutson) loaned us H.M.S. Pioneer, ...

As *Southern Cross* climbed away from Suva to the south-west, Ulm passed a message through to Warner to transmit to *The Sun*.

> Well here we are on the way again with everything running OK. In 19 or 20 hours we will be in dear old Aussie again. Our landing in Brisbane will be the culmination of 10 months hard work and the realization of Smithy's and my ambitions to be first to really cross the Pacific by air. After arrival in Brisbane will leave next day for Sydney by air but pleasure [sic] assure Brisbane public that we intend returning there on tour after a couple of weeks rest. Cheerio all, CTP Ulm KHAB

After relaying the message, Warner probably tossed the handwritten original on the floor where it worked its way between the boards. It later ended up in the possession of Lachlan Gole, a Sydney man whose father claimed to have 'done some work on Smithy's plane'. Gole discovered the note among his father's possessions in 2009 and would have discarded it as rubbish had he not recalled seeing the name 'Ulm' recently in the press, in connection with Ulm's 88-year-old son John. Gole gave the note to John, who added it to his family's papers at the National Library of Australia. Much of the Library's collection relating to Ulm and Kingsford Smith shares similar provenance. Our national collections representing these two remarkable Australians have gradually grown over the years, as more and more material emerges from the private holdings of the many people whose lives briefly brushed up against theirs.

The message Ulm had Warner transmit to The Sun shortly after leaving Suva. The neat, ink handwriting and HMCS Pioneer stationery suggest he wrote it while staying on the Fijian government launch off the coast at Naselai.

Now confident of the flight's success, Ulm also had Warner announce the identity of their chief benefactor: 'We could never have made this flight without the generosity and wonderful help given us by Captain G. Allan Hancock of Los Angeles, California'. The announcement attributed Hancock with helping them in ways they could not explain in detail at this stage but that they wanted to publicly acknowledge him 'in the most modern manner—that is, by radio, from the first aeroplane crossing the Pacific Ocean'. The announcement thrust Hancock, who had kept his benevolent involvement private, immediately into the limelight. He was

Kingsford Smith flies Southern Cross *from New Zealand back to Sydney on 29 March 1934 following a summer barnstorming tour. This is one among very few known air-to-air photographs of* Southern Cross.

intensely embarrassed with the sudden and overwhelming media attention and did his best to deflect it, arguing that he had no interest in profits, only assisting the achievement of what he considered a worthwhile scientific goal.

Warner was part way through transmitting a similar acknowledgement of Sidney Myer's financial assistance when the generator, spinning outside the port fuselage, stripped its pinion gear and failed. That made it all three legs on which Warner had lost the ability to charge both batteries and hence, use his wireless set to both send and receive. 'I was getting used to doing with only one generator and almost forgot to cuss', he recalled.

Since take-off, Lyon had been having technical problems of his own (and indeed, of his own making). The Earth Inductor Compass, he discovered, was providing a different reading to his three other compasses. 'Changing course

all the while to find out what is wrong', logged Ulm an hour after take-off. He concluded that the compass had been 'inadvertently damaged' on the beach and instructed Lyon to rely on his two 'standard' steering compasses and to check these against the Aperiodic compass, which, mounted in an immense frame, was supposed to be less subject to interference from metallic objects in the cabin and the effects of turbulence than standard compasses. Kingsford Smith later admitted that the Earth Inductor Compass' demise resulted from negligence. Before leaving Naselai, Lyon had forgotten to oil its complex mechanical innards.

These technical hitches appear not to have dampened the crew's spirits during the final afternoon's flying. Ulm described a feeling of 'unbounded confidence' regarding the journey ahead. At 1,700 kilometres it was substantially shorter than the previous two legs, seeming, commented Ulm, 'quite short to us now hardened veterans'. Navigation was easier too, their route crossing an obvious reference point (New Caledonia) and in any case, the Australian coastline being difficult to miss. Reports from the Commonwealth meteorologist were fair ('increasing cloud and some showers') and the Royal Australian Navy had dispatched HMAS *Anzac* to patrol the waters beneath their flight path. Warner summed up the feeling aboard *Southern Cross* that Friday afternoon when he recalled thinking 'what a simple matter it had been to fly across the Pacific' and pondering why nobody had done it before.

As the sun began to set, Kingsford Smith began climbing. In the log, Ulm noted how although the temperature began to drop, prompting them to climb into their fur-lined overalls, the weather ahead appeared clear. By 6.15 pm they had reached their nighttime cruising altitude of 4,300 feet. The sun had disappeared, the darkness once again throwing the hot exhaust fumes into brilliant relief. A gentle southerly breeze cut across their course but hardly affected their speed. 'This is the best night so far', declared Ulm in the log.

At this point there is a 'silence' in the log, lasting almost five hours. Resuming his commentary at 11.07 pm, Ulm explained that they had been through the most violent storm of the entire flight. Unable to climb above it, they were forced to plough right through a maelstrom of gale-force winds, torrential rain and lightning. At times, the turbulence had been so severe that it took the strength of

both pilots to hold *Southern Cross* in level flight. Thus was Ulm's brief recap of the 'worst 2½ hours on whole flight'. For a more detailed picture of what happened, and to appreciate the precarious position of *Southern Cross* for those few hours, it is necessary to turn to other sources.

Just before 7 pm, the crew had noticed a change in the weather. The temperature plummeted and the moon became obscured by clouds. Kingsford Smith recalled 'the visibility, which a short time before had enabled us to see to the distant horizon, dwindled to a mile, then to a few yards, then to nothing'. In a radio transmission, Ulm mentioned the deteriorating weather but maintained his cheery outlook.

Cheerio everybody! It wont be too long now. Possibility of fairly dirty weather tonight hence self will relieve Smithy at controls now that he may be better rested for night flying. We are as happy as Larry up here Cooee. Signed ULM KHAB

Over the next hour, the gentle southerly crosswind grew stronger, Ulm recalling in his memoir how it began to hit *Southern Cross* with gusts that 'bumped and rocked us'. He described how the stars disappeared and 'dark fingers of black clouds streaked everywhere'. Lyon's navigational charts record how their average speed dropped from 160 kilometres per hour down to about 100 kilometres per hour.

Just after 8.30 pm they hit the front of an immense storm cell. Ulm described how it struck with 'deafening force' and tossed *Southern*

The final log pages appeared in The Sun *and its associated newspapers on Sunday, 10 June 1928, shortly after* Southern Cross *landed in Sydney.*

Cross about, so that in 'a somewhat terrifying void it dropped, pitched and plunged'. The gut-churning gravitational forces produced by these sudden altitude changes caused the crew's unattached wicker chairs to float and bounce around the cabin. Opening the throttles, Kingsford Smith put the aircraft into the most rapid climb he could manage, watching the gauges carefully to stay above stalling speed. It was, reckoned Ulm, 'a supreme test in instrument flying'. In his published account of the flight he took readers into the cockpit during that slow, frightening ascent:

To look though the wind-shield was practically the same as peering through glass at a rushing cascade of water. We were enfolded in blackness. Usually, we could not see the propeller ahead. Its speed made it invisible. But now it was wet and glistening in the lash of the storm. Our little light illuminating the instrument board reflected slightly on the streaming glass, and there before us the propeller for the first time in 5500 miles made its presence known. From the centre flashed a glistening disc, the sole relief in the impenetrable blackness ahead.

Lightning bolts provided intermittent glimpses of the furious storm enveloping them. 'It ripped a hole in the clouds, revealed great masses of nimbus cloud and shot across the sky in awe-inspiring jags', remembered Kingsford Smith. He would later describe it as the worst flying of his career to date, which at that stage totalled some 3,400 hours. As evidence he would point to the propeller blades, which the rain sheared down by half an inch (13 millimetres).

Arriving at almost 8,000 feet they found no reprieve. At this point, explained Ulm, all they could do was, 'sit tight, hang grimly to the controls and keep the nose of *Southern Cross* pointed unswervingly in the direction which the instruments … told us was straight ahead'. To their disbelief, the altimeter registered changes in altitude of up to 400 feet at a time. It played havoc with their senses. Ulm described how he regularly felt that they were diving, only to see in the dim light on the instrument panel that their nose was still pointed above the horizon. He claimed that one needed remarkable discipline to trust the instruments and disregard all sensations. It must have been especially terrifying for Warner and Lyon in the blacked-out rear cabin. 'Lyon and I held on and wondered whether we were flying or falling', said Warner, while Lyon admitted to thinking the wings might collapse at any moment.

The seals around the windshield gave way and water poured into the cockpit, soaking Kingsford Smith and Ulm. 'The cold grew more and more intense', wrote Ulm, 'and our feet and hands felt like clumsy blocks of ice'. The temperature affected the engines too. After a couple of hours at their maximum ceiling their 'vital signs' began to fade, forcing Kingsford Smith to descend in a series of zooming dives, which both warmed the engines and reduced turbulence. Back at 4,400 feet just after 11 pm, they found a break in the weather and Ulm finally had a chance to resume the log.

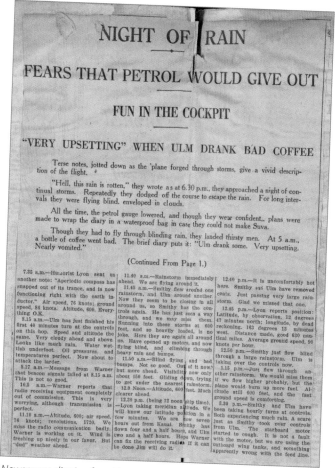

Newspaper clipping from Harry Lyon's personal scrapbook of American and Australian newspapers relating to the 1928 trans-Pacific flight.

Crowds converge on Southern Cross *after the landing at Eagle Farm aerodrome, Brisbane, 9 June 1928.*

Since 3 pm that Friday afternoon, Australians had tuned in to hear live relays of *Southern Cross'* radio transmissions. As well as Warner's hourly position updates, they heard Ulm's more detailed bulletins, including his acknowledgement of Hancock's contribution. After his jovial message at 6.50 pm mentioning the possibility of 'fairly dirty weather', however, Australian listeners heard little else for several hours. Once *Southern Cross* hit the storm, Ulm instructed Warner not to report it. 'It would worry our people to death. Will tell you should things become very serious.' In any case, the turbulence, which tossed the two Americans about the rear cabin, prevented Warner from working his key. For most of the night he left it screwed down to transmit a continuous tone, a signal they were still airborne. To families gathered around their wireless sets, *Southern Cross'* transmissions came through as demented and incoherent shrieks and whines. To an experienced wireless operator like Charlie Hodge, still listening in from USS *Omaha's* radio room, the noises painted a disconcerting picture. 'Call shrieked with violent pitch', he logged at one stage. 'I think plane has evidently plunged downward through the storm. They seem to be in very bumpy air as generators speed up and down.'

Between midnight and 3.30 am, *Southern Cross* encountered a succession of thunderstorms. In the log Ulm explained how for four hours they had 'been dodging up and down at altitudes between 500 and 9000 feet', though he reckoned none of these subsequent storms had the intensity of the first. Being drenched made the hours before sunrise 'miserably uncomfortable'. They had no gloves; Ulm apologised to future readers of the log for making so few entries. 'Hands too numb to write now.'

At that time of year the southern hemisphere was in the midst of winter. Travelling 'with' the night, darkness lasted almost 13 hours for the crew of *Southern Cross*. At half-past seven (ship's time) the sky finally paled and the clouds thinned enough for them to make out the white caps on the ocean below. 'Dawn is just breaking', logged Ulm. 'My feet are like blocks of ice, and I'd give a finger for a smoke. Believe we will sight the Aussie Coast within two hours.'

'ON OUR WAY HOME'

Reception in Australia, 9–16 June 1928

10.00
am   Left Eagle Farm - farewell by
Mayor & thousands people.
Take off about 450feet. 250galls -
Revs in air 1800 - ~~down & two~~
Circled crowd - Turned throttled back
to 1600 Revs.

10.05   Alt 1000 - Airspeed 75K. Revs 1575
we are on our way home,

10.00am Left Eagle Farm—Farewell by Mayor thousands people.

Take off about 450 feet—250 galls—

Revs in air 1800—

Circled crowd— ? throttled back to 1600 Revs

10.05 Alt 1000—Airspeed 75k. Revs 1575

We are on our way home

'It was all Smithy and Ulm's flight': Southern Cross taxies at Eagle Farm after touching down, 9 June 1928. Warner and Lyon (right background) have left the aircraft, intending to make a quiet exit.

Ulm recalled how the rising sun produced 'a comforting warmth penetrating our soaking bodies'. Using it to take a sextant shot, Lyon was surprised to calculate they were more or less where they should have been, about 270 kilometres south-east of Brisbane. The storm had knocked his sextant around severely, though, and he couldn't be certain of its accuracy. With a dead receiver battery, Warner had no hope of raising a land-based station to confirm their position. Considering they could hardly miss Australia in any case, Kingsford Smith simply headed west.

As the sun came up the clouds disappeared, revealing a bright winter's day. At 9.50 am, Ulm perceived a 'long grey shadow' on the western horizon. As the minutes passed, hills and a sea cliff appeared to spring up from the ocean. 'Loud cheers', scribbled Ulm in the log. 'Our goal is in sight. In an hour or so we will have satisfied our ambition to be the first ones to cross the Pacific by air.' Reflecting on the moment six years later, he would consider it the greatest of his life.

Kingsford Smith immediately knew they were off course, having not spotted Moreton Island, 'the airman's landmark for Brisbane'. As they crossed the coast, Ulm recognised Ballina, his wife Jo's hometown. *Southern Cross* had made landfall 140 kilometres south of its intended destination, an indication of the storm's intensity. They turned north, and were shortly met by a formation of seven aircraft from Brisbane, come to escort them in.

The Brisbane suburb of Auchenflower, as it appeared in 1928.

Southern Cross *touches down at Eagle Farm, 10.50 am, Saturday 9 June 1928. Since leaving Oakland ten days earlier it had been in the air for almost 82 hours and covered some 12,000 kilometres.*

The greatest moment of his life: Ulm climbs from the cockpit of Southern Cross *at Eagle Farm aerodrome.*

An hour later, *Southern Cross* passed over the unpainted corrugated iron roofs of Brisbane's south-eastern suburbs. About 8 kilometres to the city's north-east, Kingsford Smith could clearly pick out Eagle Farm's large iron hangars 'winking like heliographs' in the morning sun. A sea of people—some 15,000—had gathered in a semi-circle around the tarmac and cars covered the surrounding paddocks and roads stretching back towards the city.

Kingsford Smith circled the aerodrome twice before landing. 'It was a wonderful and never-to-be forgotten sight', reported one journalist. 'The crowd went wild.' *Southern Cross* taxied across the field and pulled up before the police cordon with Kingsford Smith waving from the cockpit. He and Ulm descended 'into a surging press of people', all intent on congratulating them personally.

Kingsford Smith greeted the crowd with 'Hello Aussies—my kingdom for a smoke'; and in the next instant both airmen were drawing heavily on cigarettes in 'luxurious enjoyment'. With difficulty, the police hauled the two grimy faced Australians through the crowd to a dais where the official welcoming party waited.

What about the Americans? *The Sun* reported that they emerged from the cabin after Kingsford Smith and Ulm wearing dapper blue suits. That they were wearing the dinner suits purchased in Suva is beyond doubt from the photographs, but we can be certain that they did not leave the plane in the manner reported by *The Sun*. Warner and Lyon had, in fact, exited *Southern Cross* as Kingsford Smith taxied slowly towards the enclosure; a fact unwittingly caught by a photographer. As Lyon explained during a radio interview in

'My kingdom for a smoke': Unchecked by the police, the crowd hoists Kingsford Smith aloft at Eagle Farm.

1958, 'Jim and I had the intention as soon as we got there—it was all Smithy and Ulm's flight—that we'd disappear. So we got out of the plane and started for the fence'. They didn't get far, as one journalist reported, 'when the crowd pounced on them with a cheer and hoisted them shoulder high. Moments later they were thrust onto the rickety dais with Kingsford Smith and Ulm to great cheers and shouts of "Look, it's the Yanks" and "Look at him. He's the boy who worked the keys"'.

During the official speeches the completely inadequate police force—just 90 officers—lost control of the seething mass of spectators. They surged against the dais, causing it to collapse; radio equipment and cameras were trampled and the police 'swept away like straws in the wind'. The throng carried the four fliers to an open-top car, which after a circuit of the field headed for town, passing the north Brisbane suburb of Hamilton where Kingsford Smith had been born. By one estimate 30,000 people were crammed onto Queen and Adelaide Streets to welcome the airmen. They swarmed around the motorcade and leaned from every available balcony and window. Girls shouted 'Kingy you darling!' and showered the airmen—still wearing flying caps and wet overalls—with flowers. At Town Hall, the Mayor gave a speech, proclaiming the flight a watershed in aviation history. He read a congratulatory telegram from the Prime Minister, and an announcement that the federal government had awarded the party £5,000.

'Kingy you darling!': An estimated 30,000 people crammed into Brisbane's centre to capture a glimpse of the fliers as they made their way to a civic reception at Town Hall.

The four airmen then replied, Kingsford Smith and Ulm emphasising the team effort and piling accolades on the Americans. Lyon and Warner briefly expressed gratitude, but appeared uncomfortable with the attention.

As per the contract they had signed in Suva, Warner and Lyon were supposed to leave *Southern Cross* in Brisbane. The day after their arrival, however, *The Sun* reported that 'at a midnight conference', Kingsford Smith and Ulm had once again, in an act of sportsmanship invited the Americans to accompany them to Sydney, which

represented the journey's real conclusion. Yet again, however, it appears that in the name of decorum *The Sun* had obscured the facts.

One of *The Sun*'s competitors, *The Guardian*, had sent journalist Norman Ellison to Brisbane to cover *Southern Cross'* arrival. That afternoon he ran into Lyon in the lounge at Lennon's Hotel, and struck up a conversation. Ellison was surprised to learn that the Americans would not be flying to Sydney and that Lyon had fallen out with Ulm while drunk in Suva. Perceiving a potential scoop, Ellison approached Ulm and Kingsford Smith's minders with a threat: if the

Kingsford Smith and Ulm embraced their honorary status as Royal Australian Air Force officers, though not everyone in the small, recently established and highly competitive service embraced them. The air force's leadership ordered Ulm to remove his pilot's 'wings' as he had no official flying qualifications.

Americans did not accompany *Southern Cross* to Sydney, *The Guardian* would charter an aircraft for them and report Lyon and Ulm's argument. They had 30 minutes to decide. As Ellison related,

Ten minutes later, the secretary came back to the lounge—several other reporters had arrived—and said Smithy and Ulm would like the Press to come to their room. There Ulm was the spokesman. He said there seemed to be a story around that the two Americans were being left in Brisbane. Not so, he declared; they were coming to Sydney in the Southern Cross.

'One mad exciting whirl'

Southern Cross left Eagle Farm the following morning, Sunday, 10 June 1928. The Mayor, along with thousands of Queenslanders, turned out to farewell the Pacific fliers. After circling the aerodrome and waving, Kingsford Smith set a southerly course. 'We are on our way home', noted Ulm in the log.

Approaching Sydney on that Sunday afternoon, it seemed to Kingsford Smith that 'the entire population … had either assembled at Mascot Aerodrome, or was on its way

'On our way home': The crew of Southern Cross *say farewell to their hosts at Eagle Farm on 10 June 1928 before embarking for Sydney—the journey's symbolic ending.*

When Southern Cross flew over Sydney Harbour on 10 June 1928, construction on the bridge pylons had just begun. Bennelong Point, future site of the Opera House, can be seen at upper left, at the foot of the Botanic Gardens.

there'. Whereas they had expected 'a quiet little crowd' of around 10,000, something like 200,000 people—about one in six of all the city's residents—had gathered to welcome 'their' airmen home. Nothing like the major international airport it is today, in 1928 the aerodrome at Mascot—which would later adopt Kingsford Smith's name—was not yet a decade old. Surrounded by marshland and connected to Sydney's then-distant city centre by rough roads it was, in effect, an often-waterlogged paddock surrounded by a few small huts and hangars.

Following the crowd management debacle in Brisbane, New South Wales police had made far more extensive arrangements. Four hundred officers kept the spectators at bay and formed a phalanx astride *Southern Cross* as it taxied in. They efficiently ushered the crew onto a stage where an official party, including Kingsford Smith's parents and Ulm's wife, waited. After a brief introduction by the Governor General, the airmen made a circuit of the aerodrome on the back of a lorry before retiring into the New South Wales Aero Club hut for a private afternoon tea. Most spectators went away from the brief proceedings profoundly disappointed, the luckiest having only caught a fleeting glimpse of their heroes.

The unprecedented attention *Southern Cross'* crew received in Sydney is evidence of the significance that ordinary people attributed to the event and the immense pride they felt for what they considered a national achievement. The trans-Pacific flight occurred at a time in which Australians, aware that they had sacrificed much in the Great War, believed they should play a larger part in world affairs. The Pacific flight both validated this view and provided an example of Australians making a highly visible contribution on the world stage.

On a more pragmatic level, however, people turned out in such immense numbers at Mascot and Eagle Farm because of the innovative manner in which the press had reported the flight. Never before had news coverage been so immediate and engaging. As one anonymous 'ordinary wage earner' wrote to *The Sun*, the live radio coverage had left him 'shaken to the depths at times'. When *Southern Cross* landed safely in Brisbane, he ran next door and found his neighbours gathered around their wireless, also in the throes of emotion. Together they went to the pub and 'with many others drank to the health, happiness and prosperity of those aerial giants'. Warner's radio transmissions and

In contrast with the shambolic, and indeed dangerous, reception in Brisbane, an ample police presence ensured the tight, efficient management of Southern Cross' *arrival at Mascot.*

the excerpts of Ulm's log published by *The Sun* had allowed Australians to experience the flight vicariously. Meeting the airmen 'in person' represented a logical ending to a journey in which they felt they had all participated.

The crew of *Southern Cross* remained in Sydney for three nights, subject to a whirlwind of social engagements. The city hosted them at a civic reception at the Town Hall and paraded them through the centre of Sydney. *The Sun* and the Lord Mayor each hosted a lunch at the Hotel Australia on Castlereagh Street, while the Returned Sailors' and Soldiers' Imperial League of Australia (RSSILA) and the Aero Club held separate dinners in their honour. In between, they did wreath-laying ceremonies, radio interviews and attended theatre shows. Warner and Lyon joined in, the Australian public perceiving them not as salaried assistants but partners in a remarkable achievement. Discerning the weight of popular expectation, Ulm announced they would continue with *Southern Cross* to Melbourne.

The day they arrived in Sydney, George Allan Hancock cabled from the United States, presenting *Southern Cross* to Ulm and Kingsford Smith as a gift. Hancock's considerable generosity effectively cleared their personal debt. This did not, however, stop the public showering them with gifts; nor did it stop organisations such as the RSSILA and various newspapers raising prize money for the airmen. On their third day in Sydney, for example, the party attended a performance at the Prince Edward Theatre where the management presented a £100 cheque and wireless radio sets from the Altwater Kent Company. They received another £5,000 that night at a dinner hosted by the Aero Club. A few days later in Melbourne Vacuum Oil Co. pledged £4,500 and it was rumoured that Lebbeus Hordern, of the wealthy Hordern retailing family, pitched in another £5,000. Still more would come from Canberra's ex-servicemen later in the week. It is uncertain how much Kingsford Smith and Ulm received in total, though it almost certainly exceeded £30,000—equivalent to about A$2 million today. There were other accolades too; Kingsford Smith and Ulm both received honourary commissions in the Royal Australian Air Force and an Air Force Cross, with an American National Geographic Society Medal and a trophy from the Fédération Aéronautique Internationale following. Rumours abounded that they would be knighted.

Public opinion was practically unanimous: the Pacific fliers deserved the rewards. Some even criticised the federal government for its 'paltry' contribution, compared with that from other sources. According to letters to the editor, the public also overwhelmingly believed that Lyon and Warner deserved an equal share. They had undertaken the same risks and, in any case, one of their countrymen's generosity had made the venture possible in the first place. The issue even came up in parliament, the opposition pressing the Prime Minister to stipulate that Kingsford Smith and Ulm share the government's

Stay back! Police rush to form a guard around Southern Cross *after it touches down at Mascot aerodrome.*

The crew of Southern Cross face the press on the official dais at Mascot, 10 June 1928.

Jim Warner starting the starboard motor of Southern Cross before take-off to Melbourne from Sydney.

award equally with Lyon and Warner. American
newspapers raised the question too, although they
generally assumed, as *The San Francisco Examiner* did,
that Kingsford Smith and Ulm being 'the best of
good sports will doubtlessly divide the bounty with
the crew'. Feeling the squeeze of public opinion
again, Ulm attempted to end the speculation with a
statement to the press. He somewhat misleadingly
claimed that there had been 'the utmost harmony
and comradeship' between the four men throughout
the journey and announced that he and Kingsford
Smith had offered the Americans an equal share, but
that they had declined to accept it.

Warner later denied this, noting somewhat ruefully
in his memoir, that 'to be perfectly truthful I would
have liked to have burdened myself down with
a dollar or two of this "filthy lucre"'. He claimed
that, in fact, he and Lyon had received numerous
offers of gifts but could not accept them because of
the contracts they had signed. Warner urged Ulm
to release them, but he refused for ten days, 'by
which time it was too late'. The Americans would
leave Australia empty handed, though they would
share US$12,000 raised by Hearst Newspapers.
It represented the equivalent of about half what
Ulm and Kingsford Smith had received from the
Commonwealth government alone. Ulm's ruthless
approach to upholding the contracts is certainly
not endearing, but it cannot be said to have been
unethical or illegal. He simply held Lyon and
Warner to the unequivocal conditions under which
he had employed them. Ulm's apparent dishonesty
to the press, however, is more difficult to excuse.

*Ulm's wife Jo (left) and Kingsford Smith's parents Catherine and William
greeted the party at Mascot, ending almost a year of separation.*

The weight of public and press opinion demanded the Americans join Kingsford Smith and Ulm for the publicity tour.

Southern Cross flew to Melbourne on Wednesday, 13 June, some 50,000 people seeing it off from Mascot aerodrome. Along with the Americans, Kingsford Smith's mother and Ulm's wife came along for the ride. Six hours later, they landed at Essendon aerodrome with an escort of 14 Royal Australian Air Force aircraft and before an audience of 100,000 spectators. For almost 8 kilometres, cars gridlocked Flemington Road, creating worse traffic jams than Melbourne typically experienced on Cup Day. An official party including the Premier and the war hero Lieutenant General Sir John Monash greeted the fliers at a well-managed event at the aerodrome before they were whisked off to

a dinner at the Menzies Hotel hosted by one of the flight's sponsors, Vacuum Oil Co.

The crew of *Southern Cross* and their guests spent the following day in Melbourne being feted at separate functions hosted by the Governor, the Lord Mayor and the RSSILA. A body with considerable political influence in Australia during the 1920s, Australia's ex-service establishment had strongly advocated the flight since its inception, lobbying the government to provide financial support and leading fundraising initiatives throughout the country. In return, Kingsford Smith and Ulm provided the RSSILA with an embodiment of what it called 'the digger spirit', which validated the ex-service group's enduring importance in society and the dominance of 'Anzac' and 'digger' for Australian national identity.

Southern Cross departed for Canberra on Friday morning, 15 June. True to form, the battery generators on the aircraft's fuselage gave trouble, though this time the culprit was the starboard unit, which ironically had provided reliable service throughout the journey. Flying over Melbourne, Warner had instructions to drop, on Ulm's signal, a wreath over the Shrine of Remembrance, on which construction had recently commenced. Putting his arm outside the cockpit when the moment arrived, Ulm accidentally hit the spinning generator, bending one of its blades. The generator began vibrating so severely that as they flew over the city's outskirts, Ulm passed a message to Warner instructing him to cut the damaged unit free. Leaning out the cabin window with a hacksaw, Warner obeyed, despite having an 'awful feeling' that it might hit something—or somebody. Aside from taking some skin of Ulm's hand, however, the generator caused no injury, but it did break some telegraph wires and bury itself in the platform of Donnybrook railway station. The station-master resisted the temptation to keep the mangled unit as a souvenir and posted it back to Ulm and Kingsford Smith's office in Sydney.

In 1928 Canberra was still very much an isolated bush town. Although commissioned as the national capital 15 years previously, the Great War had delayed construction and by mid-1928 the town still had few permanent public buildings and a population of less than 6,000. Parliament House had opened the year before amid sheep-grazing paddocks, though many federal departments remained in Melbourne and would for some time to come.

The crowd that gathered at Duntroon aerodrome that afternoon was, as a result, much smaller than those in the state capitals, although people had come from as far afield as Goulburn, Cooma and Yass. Prime Minister Stanley Melbourne Bruce and his wife met the crew and presented them with £5,000 from the federal government. 'No man can measure the value of your achievement', he said. 'No government can adequately express the feelings of its people in face of your accomplishment.' That afternoon, the crew attended a reception at Parliament House where the vice-president of the Executive Council, Sir George Pearce, made a lengthy speech in which he quoted from the log, which Ulm had agreed to donate to the Commonwealth. The RSSILA hosted the crew for dinner at the Hotel Canberra (Lyon and Warner became 'honorary diggers') and afterwards they attended a picture show at the Capitol Theatre featuring newsreels of their arrival in Brisbane and Sydney. After the week they had experienced it must have seemed like an eternity ago, although it was only six days since *Southern Cross'* wheels had touched down at Eagle Farm and just over a fortnight since they had left Oakland.

Southern Cross returned to Sydney the next day. The Americans stayed for another week before boarding a steamer bound for San Francisco. Warner left his iconic Panama hat and Lyon his navigational charts as gifts, the latter ending up in the National Library's collection. In return the Americans accepted a pet kangaroo each, though sadly, neither animal survived long after the sea voyage. Of greater longevity would be the significance of Lyon and Warner's involvement in the flight for Australian–US relations. To Australians in the 1920s the American people seemed distant and isolated by their own self-interest; their culture had yet to supplant the inherent Britishness that still dominated the Australian outlook. The American contribution to the Pacific flight, and especially Hancock's generosity, began to erode the cultural barriers between the two nations and restore a mistrust that many Australians felt towards the United States in the aftermath of the Great War. Typical of many who wrote to newspapers on the topic, Mr W. Johnston of Lithgow admitted that American involvement in the flight had changed his opinion 'concerning America and Americans considerably' and prompted him to recognise that Australia needed the 'friendship' of the United States. Johnston reckoned 'the flight is in this way far more significant than it first seems'. It was an astute observation. Australia and the United States would become much closer in the coming decades, their mutual interest in the Pacific, as implied by

Southern Cross' flight, being brought into stark relief by the Second World War and the perceived threat of communism thereafter.

On Kingsford Smith and Ulm's arrival in Sydney, Vacuum Oil Co. had assigned the two airmen a personal secretary to handle the circus their lives had suddenly come to resemble. It was a big opportunity for Ellen Rogers, being just 21 years old and, like most Australians, having never flown before. She could not have known that her close association with the two Australian aviators—and Ulm in particular— would extend for the remainder of their lives and then, that she would devote much of the rest of her own life to preserving their memory. 'Rog', as she quickly became known in the Kingsford Smith–Ulm circle, recalled the post-flight tour as 'one mad exciting whirl'. In her date book, she counted up 57 official engagements besides 'a continual influx of visitors' in between. It had no doubt been a completely gratifying (albeit exhausting) return for the stress and danger that the two Australians had experienced in organising and then carrying out the flight. But fame and fortune did not represent an end in itself. Kingsford Smith and Ulm had in mind big things for Australian aviation. Now, with the Pacific conquered, they believed they had the means to realise their ambitions.

Lyon and Warner embark for the United States, 23 June 1928. There is no evidence they ever saw Kingsford Smith or Ulm again.

Crowds at Circular Quay farewell the Americans; their involvement contributed to a shift in Australian attitudes towards the United States.

'THE REST IS EASY'

The years beyond

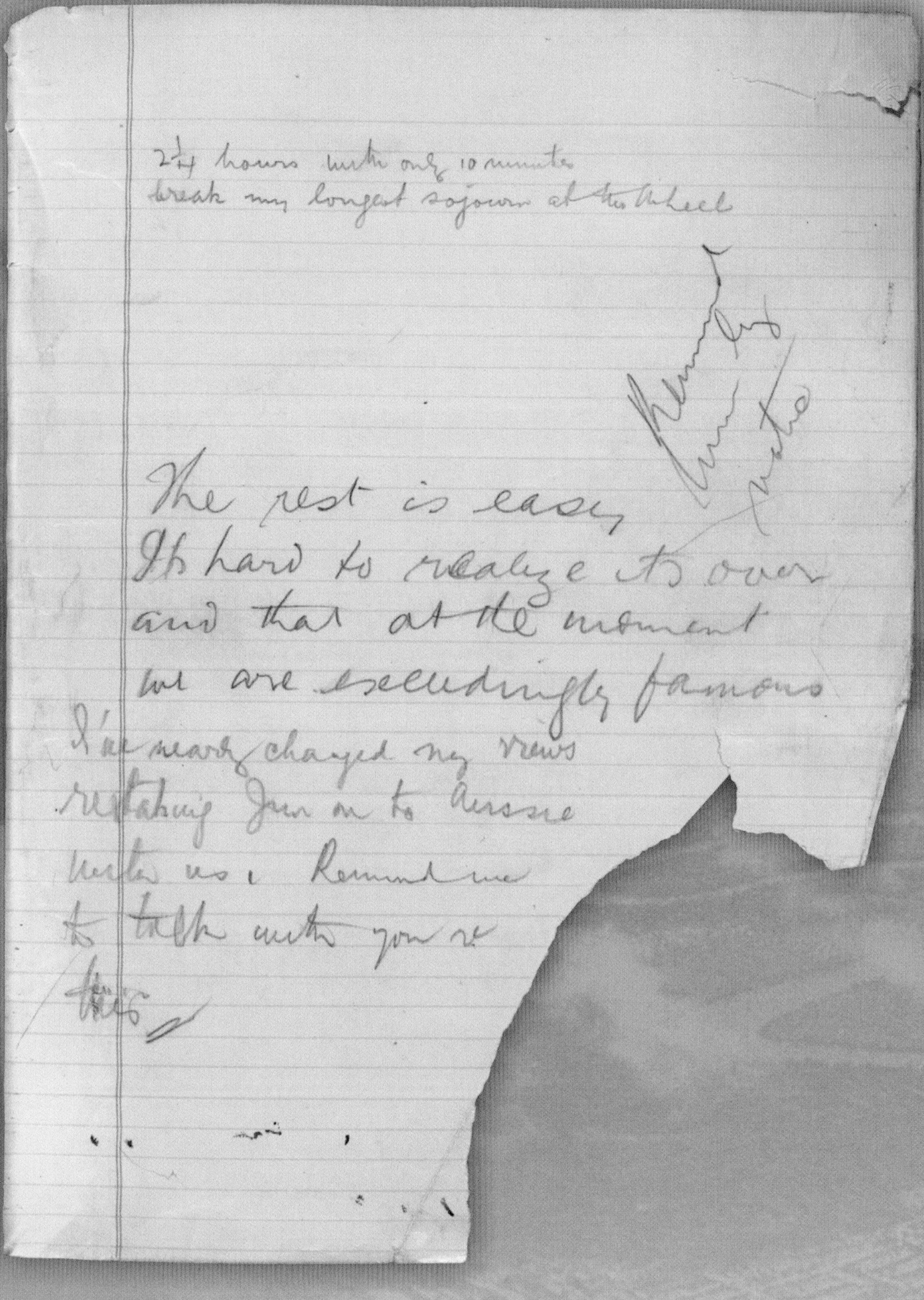

24 hours with only 10 minutes
break my longest sojourn at the wheel

The rest is easy
Its hard to realize its over
and that at the moment
we are exceedingly famous
I've nearly changed my views
retaking Jim on to Aussie
write us. Remind me
to talk with you re
this

2¼ hours with only 10 minutes break my longest sojourn at the wheel

Remind him by note

The rest is easy

Its hard to realize its over and that at the moment we are exceedingly famous

I've nearly changed my views re taking Jim on to Aussie with us. Remind me to talk with you re this.

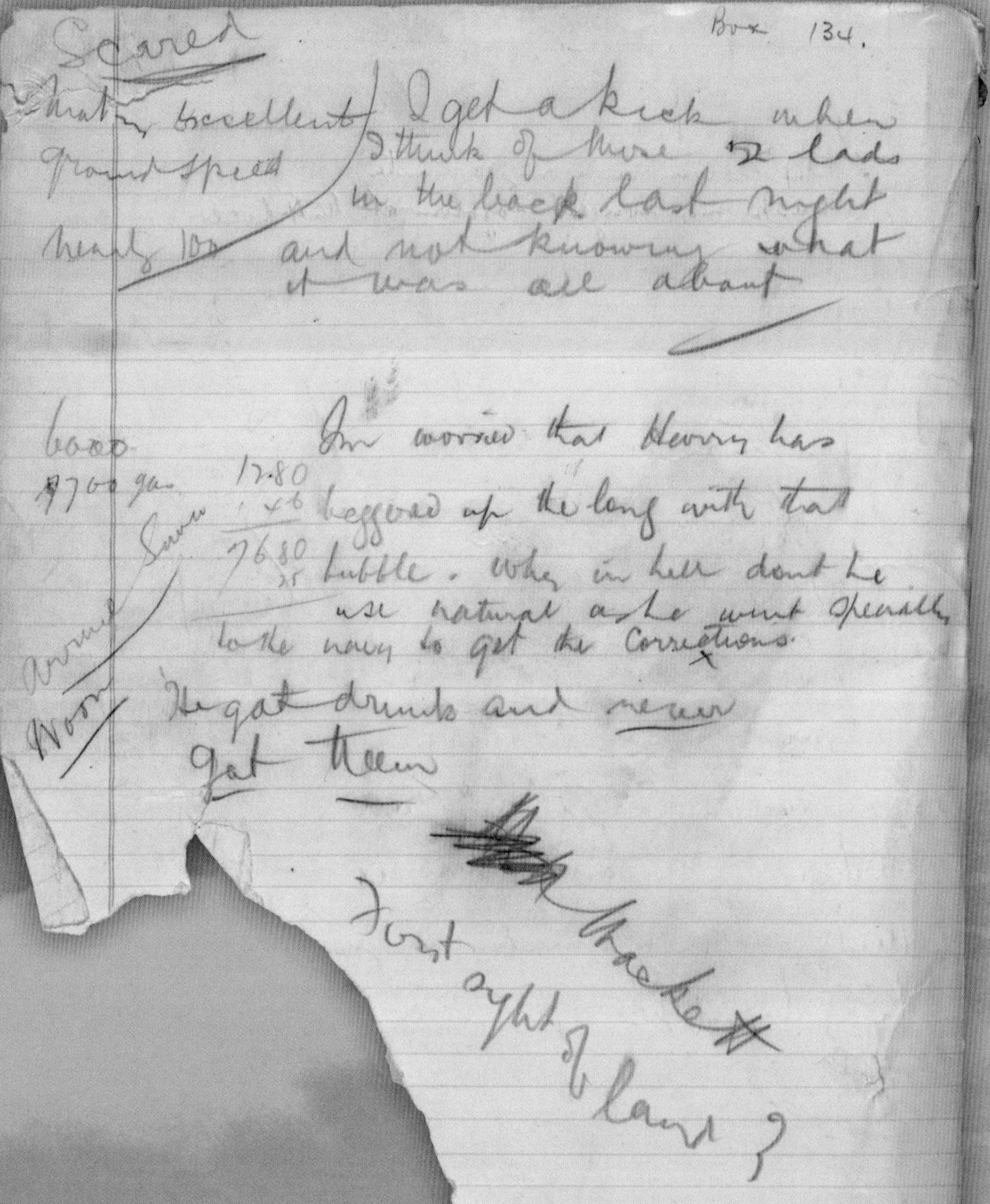

Scared

that excellent) I get a kick when
ground speed   I think of those 2 lads
                      in the back last night
nearly 100   and not knowing what
             it was all about

6000   Im worried that Kluvery has
9700 ga. 17.80
Sum   1.46 beggered up the long with that
          7680 bubble. Why in hell dont he
             25   use natural as he went specially
          to the navy to get the Corrections.
                  He got drunk and never
          get them
                    —

                          Shacks
             dont
             sight of
               island ?

Scared

Making excellent ground speed nearly 100

I get a kick when I think of those 2 lads in the back last night and not knowing what it was all about.

Arrive Suva noon

Im worried that Harry has beggared up the long with that bubble. Why in hell dont he use natural as he went specially to the navy to get the corrections.

He got drunk and never got them.

First sight of land?

The product of his second marriage, Kingsford Smith had a son, Charles Arthur, in December 1932.

In the moments following the crew's sighting of Fiji, Ulm had made a triumphant declaration to Kingsford Smith on the log's second-last page: 'The rest is easy Its hard to realize its over and that at the moment we are exceedingly famous'. By 'the rest', Ulm meant the final stretch of the Pacific flight connecting Suva with Brisbane. It was typical Ulm: energetic, upbeat and eminently confident. Yet, as we know in hindsight, the worst flying still lay ahead. *Southern Cross'* near-catastrophic encounter with an immense tropical storm front between Fiji and the Australian coast demonstrated the flaw in Ulm's optimistic outlook.

It would be entirely understandable if after touring Australia's capital cities, Ulm believed that his newfound fame and fortune assured the achievement of his and Kingsford Smith's ambitions. Yet any notion of Ulm's that smooth flying would characterise their subsequent endeavours was likewise to prove ironically and eventually tragically misplaced.

Amid the whirl of celebrations and endless public engagements in the weeks following the Pacific flight, Ulm later explained that his mind dwelt on one question: 'What next?' The public response to the Pacific flight revealed, he believed, Australia's readiness to adopt air travel as part of the national transport system. While Sydney 'went mad' around them and Kingsford Smith enjoyed being the man about town, Ulm got down to business. As Ellen Rogers later recalled of her new employers, 'Kingsford Smith I found to be a cheery, friendly man who spent a lot of time chatting to his cousins and friends, while Ulm held countless interviews between dictating letters to me'. Among those letters and interviews were the foundation of the inter-city air service Ulm hoped to establish with Kingsford Smith as his partner. It would grow, he hoped, to link Australia to Europe and America via air.

Having hired a new navigator and wireless operator, in August Kingsford Smith and Ulm made the first non-stop flight from Melbourne to Perth, completing the 3,300-kilometre journey in just under 24 hours. As well as giving the new crew experience, Ulm later admitted he intended to build publicity and demonstrate the feasibility of a trans-city air service. A month later, they flew *Southern Cross* over the Tasman in the first Australia–New Zealand flight. Although the crossing would only take 14 hours—far shorter than any of the Pacific stretches—the weather proved even more treacherous than that between Suva and Brisbane. Ice caused the radio and gauges to fail and put *Southern Cross* into an out-of-control dive at one point from which Kingsford Smith and Ulm only narrowly recovered. 'I think that night I touched the extreme of human fear', Kingsford Smith later admitted. 'Panic was very near and I almost lost my head.'

In Christchurch, *Southern Cross* received a welcome rivalling the one she had experienced at Mascot following the Pacific flight. For three weeks Kingsford Smith and

One of ANA's Avro X airliners above Sydney Harbour, early in 1931. Ulm's son John recalls watching the bridge's arches slowly coming together from his father's Dover Heights house during this time.

Ulm toured New Zealand, using the opportunity to drum up publicity and develop business contacts. Kingsford Smith made the most of the boozy celebrations, while the more earnest Ulm took some flying lessons and finally qualified for his licence.

Before the end of the year Ulm had arranged necessary finances to establish, with Kingsford Smith, Australian National Airways Limited. To purchase aircraft and hire experienced pilots, they planned to fly *Southern Cross* to Britain. Their run of incredibly good fortune came to an abrupt end, though, when their inexperienced navigator became lost in a storm over north-western Australia, forcing *Southern Cross* to land in remote country near the Glenelg River. For the next fortnight the crew survived as castaways before being rescued, the result of a publicly funded search effort.

In a tragically ironic twist, one of the search party aircraft also went missing: it had been flown by Kingsford Smith and Ulm's ex-partners Keith Anderson and Bob Hitchcock. Following the Pacific flight they had unsuccessfully attempted to sue for shares in the venture's profits. Remarkably, the whole episode had not completely soured the relationship and when *Southern Cross* went missing, Anderson and Hitchcock agreed to join the search. Their biplane made a forced

Souvenir handkerchief of Kingsford Smith and Ulm's flight across the Tasman to New Zealand in September 1928.

'Comfort, Safety and Speed': Passengers aboard one of ANA's inter-city service flights enjoy a picnic lunch during the five- or six-hour journey between Sydney and Brisbane.

In February 1934, Ulm carried the first official airmail from New Zealand to Australia in an attempt to secure a government contract for a regular service.

Ulm looked less than his typically dapper self after surviving two weeks in remote north-western Australia following Southern Cross' abortive flight to Britain in March 1929.

landing in the Tanami Desert and was not found for three weeks. Anderson and Hitchcock had died from exposure.

In the wake of the tragedy, newspapers in competition with *The Sun* launched a smear campaign against the *Southern Cross* crew. Allegations circulated that Ulm had planned the forced landing as a publicity stunt, something he vehemently denied, and an official inquiry later absolved him of. Nevertheless, the rumours took the sheen off the public image the aviation partnership had previously enjoyed and, in particular, tarnished Ulm's integrity as a businessman.

Three months after their disastrous first attempt, in June 1929 Kingsford Smith and Ulm flew *Southern Cross* to Britain in 12 days and 18 hours, taking three days off the record Bert Hinkler had established the previous year. For Australian National Airways they purchased five Avro X aircraft, a near identical design to *Southern Cross*, and hired pilots, most of them ex-war fliers who, like Kingsford Smith, had cut their teeth over the Western Front a decade earlier.

Australian National Airways started daily services between Brisbane and Sydney on 1 January 1930. For the return journey, which took around eight hours, passengers paid £18 17 shillings and sixpence, about the equivalent of A$1,300 today. Despite the premium ticket prices and the developing financial Depression, Australian National Airways initially did a healthy trade, carrying 1,244 passengers during the service's first three months. At the beginning of June it added a Sydney to Melbourne route and then, in January 1931, a service to Tasmania.

Finding the daily route flying monotonous and still hoping to complete a circumnavigation in *Southern Cross*, in early 1930 Kingsford Smith planned a trans-Atlantic flight. Ulm intended to join him, but the company directors ordered him not to go. He sold his half of *Southern Cross* to Kingsford Smith for Australian National Airways shares. It foreshadowed the breaking of their partnership; they would not fly together again.

In June 1930, with a crew hired in Britain, Kingsford Smith flew *Southern Cross* over the Atlantic, from Ireland to the United States, via Newfoundland. He then flew across the American continent to San Francisco, becoming the first airman to circumnavigate the globe by a route crossing both hemispheres. Returning to Britain, Kingsford Smith purchased a single-seat Avro Avian and named it *Southern Cross Junior*. He flew it back to Australia in just under ten days, shaving a third off Hinkler's solo record. The press proclaimed him 'the greatest long distance flyer in the world' and the RAAF appointed him an honorary Air Commodore. In December, with Ulm as his groomsman, Kingsford Smith married Mary Powell, daughter of a wealthy Melbourne entrepreneur who he had met on a sea voyage the year before.

After a reasonably promising first year, things turned bad for Australian National Airways. In March 1931, *Southern Cloud* crashed in the Snowy Mountains en route from Sydney to Melbourne, killing six passengers and two pilots. The disaster, combined with the deepening economic crisis, forced the company's directors to suspend daily services. Ulm attempted to revive business by organising a Christmas airmail to Britain. He secured ample public and official support for the venture, but it turned into a costly disappointment when *Southern Sun*, carrying the mail, had an accident in Malaya. A relief aircraft flown by Kingsford Smith 'rescued' the mail and completed the journey, but in Britain this machine was also damaged, delaying the return mail until well after Christmas and topping off a rough year.

The pressures of 1931 strained Kingsford Smith and Ulm's relationship. Despite its intimate portrayal in the media, their association was fundamentally about business while personally they shared very little in common. The airline's collapse and Kingsford Smith's general lack of interest in commercial affairs created distance between the two airmen. Then, in November 1931 when Kingsford Smith's ghost-written autobiography began to be published in serialised form, Ulm was angered by what he perceived as insufficient acknowledgement in the text. Lawyers became involved, securing Ulm the right to amend Kingsford Smith's manuscript. Their colleagues recalled that subsequently they were seldom seen together.

The suspension of Australian National Airways' services forced Kingsford Smith back onto the barnstorming circuit in 1932 to make a living. For most of the year he toured country towns with, as one newspaper put it, 'his historic airliner', or 'the old bus', as he affectionately referred to *Southern Cross*. The monotony of joy-rides was broken only by the announcement of his knighthood in June and the birth of his first son, Charles, in December. Some in the ever-fickle press once again turned on Kingsford Smith, commenting that barnstorming was an unbecoming profession for a knight of the realm.

Meanwhile, Ulm spent 1932 working on proposals to save Australian National Airways from insolvency. He approached the government to subsidise a joint venture between several Australian airlines for an Australia to Singapore service to link up with an Imperial Airways Limited route to Britain. Behind the scenes, the British company lobbied the Australian government, besmirching Ulm's name. He missed out on the contract and in February 1933, Australian National Airways went into voluntary liquidation.

In his indomitable way, just days after news of the company's collapse, Ulm announced the formation of a new company, British International Airlines Limited, to bid for the Australia–Singapore route. It would be a 'wholly Australian' enterprise, using local capital, pilots, mechanics and, where possible, Australian-manufactured equipment. Ulm invested all his personal finances in the purchase of one of the old Australian National Airways Avros and dubbed it *Faith in Australia*. To prove his point—that Australia did not have to rely on international expertise—he planned a global circumnavigation tour and hired ex-Australian National Airways pilots Scotty Allan and Bill Taylor as crew.

Ulm left for Britain in *Faith in Australia* on 21 June 1933 but, disappointingly, engine trouble prevented them breaking any records; the journey took 17 days. For the second leg, Ulm planned to follow Kingsford Smith's 1930 route and fly across the Atlantic, from Portmarnock Beach in Ireland to Newfoundland. Preparations went smoothly until just a few hours before take-off. While being refuelled on the beach, *Faith in Australia*'s undercarriage collapsed, badly damaging the aircraft. Through good fortune, a British philanthropist interested in aviation funded the repairs, but by the time they were finished favourable flying weather over the north Atlantic had passed for the year.

Kingsford Smith was also in Britain at this time. Bored with a second year of barnstorming, he had gone there and purchased a Percival Gull (*Miss Southern Cross*) to attempt to break the latest Britain to Australia solo record. Starting on 4 October 1933 he reached Wyndham in Western Australia in just over seven days, taking almost two days off British aviator Charles Scott's previous record. Thirty thousand people greeted Kingsford Smith's return to Sydney

Premier Bertram Stevens christens Ulm's plane Faith in Australia in 1933.

and the government awarded him £3,000—the equivalent of over A$250,000 today.

In the repaired *Faith in Australia*, Ulm and his crew left Britain nine days after Kingsford Smith. Although dogged by mechanical problems and atrocious weather, Ulm managed to beat his old colleague's new record by almost 11 hours. The press lauded Ulm, calling for his knighthood, but there were no official rewards forthcoming. Nonetheless, he graciously told reporters that his and Kingsford Smith's flights couldn't be compared. 'One was an extraordinary individual effort, while three pilots had shared in the success of the *Faith in Australia*.'

Ulm's record of achievements failed to convince the government that an all-Australian company could run the service to Singapore. In April 1934 the contract went to Qantas Empire Airways, a partnership between Imperial Airways and Qantas. Ulm thereafter returned to the formidable ambition he had harboured in 1928 of establishing a trans-Pacific service. In September he invested all his personal assets in yet another company, Great Pacific Airways Limited. Embarking for Britain, he planned to purchase an aircraft and make a demonstration flight home from America. Ulm recorded his feelings about the significance of this new venture in a short memoir that he wrote during the sea voyage.

Ulm speaks with American aviatrix Amelia Earhart at Oakland aerodrome, 3 December 1934, just before embarking on his final flight.

'I have no doubt in my own mind', he wrote, 'that I am standing at last on the threshold of vast possibilities of which I have dreamt, and for which I have worked for many years'.

The memoir would never be published and this comment would shortly after inherit a tragically ironic significance. At the beginning of December 1934, in a twin-engine Airspeed Envoy named *Stella Australis* and with an inexperienced crew hired when his regular colleagues Allan and Taylor declined to join him, Ulm made final preparations to fly from Oakland to Sydney, more or less reprising the flight that had launched his career. In San Francisco, a few days before leaving, Kingsford Smith's and Ulm's paths crossed once again. A few weeks earlier, Kingsford Smith and Taylor had crossed the Pacific in the other direction in a twin-seat Lockheed Altair named *Lady Southern Cross*. 'Ulm's old partner greeted him cordially', reported a journalist, 'and they decided to spend the remainder of the day together'.

Stella Australis took off from Oakland at 3.41 pm, Monday, 3 December 1934, bound for Honolulu. Throughout the evening, Ulm's wireless operator reported ample progress and ideal flying weather. At some stage after 2 am, however, *Stella Australis* encountered a storm, and despite climbing to 12,000 feet failed to clear it. Around dawn, the messages began to sound alarming: Ulm's navigator didn't know where they were and they had very little fuel left. Just after 9 am, *Stella Australis* began transmitting

'Standing at last on the threshold of vast possibilities': Ulm perceived his survey flight in Stella Australis *as the culmination of all his efforts.*

'SOS'. Twenty minutes later Ulm radioed that they were about to ditch in the water.

Despite a massive air and sea search, the United States Navy failed to find any trace of *Stella Australis* or her crew. When the Americans called off the search after a week, Ulm's wife chartered a schooner to search the outlying islands, following the sea currents as far as Midway. After nine months it too found nothing.

Ulm's death shocked the nation and overwhelmed his family. His son John, then 13 years old, recalls that when his mother told him the news he broke down. 'Suddenly and immensely I was devastated.' He also remembers how the tragedy brought home his father's significance. 'Walking to and from school', he explains, 'people touched me in the street—strangers, but to them not really'. The worldwide aviation community responded with an outpouring of tributes. A central figure in the nascent Australian aviation industry, Lawrence Wackett, believed Ulm 'probably the greatest living exponent of the future of aviation' but lamented that 'his country failed in its real appreciation'. Ironically, the nation's gratitude came just too late. Years later, John Ulm learned from records released by the National Archives that in December 1934 Prime Minister Joseph Lyons had recommended his father for a knighthood. It would have been announced at the flight's completion.

Ulm's death shattered Kingsford Smith, whose health, by the end of 1934 was on the verge of collapse. The strain of long-distance flying, years of heavy drinking and smoking and the fact that he was approaching 40 weighed on him. Nevertheless, financial problems forced Kingsford Smith on yet another barnstorming tour in *Southern Cross* during the early months of 1935. Business proved poor, neither he nor flying being the novelty it had been in 1928, leading him to consider more permanent ventures. As Ulm had, Kingsford Smith turned to the government for support, proposing a trans-Tasman airmail service. Lacking the business and political skills of his late colleague, he made little headway, turning instead to what he knew best: a sensational, press-hyped feat to win popular support.

Ulm bought this caricature at the Eiffel Tower when he and Kingsford Smith visited Europe in 1929 to purchase aircraft and hire crew for Australian National Airlines.

With Bill Taylor and another old flying mate, John Stannage, Kingsford Smith organised for *Southern Cross* to carry a special 'Jubilee' mail from Australia to New Zealand on 15 May 1935. What followed became one of the most celebrated incidents in the 'Smithy' legend. Six hours out over the Tasman, the exhaust on *Southern Cross'* tired old centre engine broke off, a piece of debris smashing the starboard propeller. Kingsford Smith turned the aircraft around and headed back to Sydney, hoping to make it on two engines. They did so barely, and only because Taylor climbed out of the aircraft onto a wing strut to transfer oil from the 'dud' engine into the port one, using a thermos and briefcase.

Although it provided matter for a compelling legend, the whole sorry affair can hardly have helped Kingsford Smith's business prospects, especially given that he was forced to jettison the mail over the Tasman. Apparently undeterred, in June 1935 Kingsford Smith established 'Trans Tasman Air Service' with a group of mates. Together, they could only scrape together a meagre starting capital of £575. To make ends meet, Kingsford Smith sold *Southern Cross* to the government. The best he could manage from the Lyons administration was £3,000, what he and Ulm had paid Wilkins for it minus engines and instruments eight years earlier.

Frustrated with renewed attempts to secure government backing, Kingsford Smith planned an overseas tour to raise more capital and

The briefcase Bill Taylor used to move oil between Southern Cross' *engines during the near-disastrous flight to New Zealand in May 1935.*

purchase a passenger-carrying aircraft. With Tommy Pethybridge, a young pilot he had previously worked with on barnstorming tours, Kingsford Smith went to Britain via the United States to collect *Lady Southern Cross*. He had unsuccessfully tried to sell the two-seat Lockheed Altair in America and now intended flying her back to Australia for conversion into a passenger carrier. Kingsford Smith could not

resist the temptation to make a new attempt on the Britain to Australia record, intending to beat the latest best time of just under two days.

In *Lady Southern Cross*, Kingsford Smith and Pethybridge took off from Lympne aerodrome in England in the pre-dawn dark of 6 November 1935. Kingsford Smith had been ill and a number of people, including his wife, had urged him not to fly. Nonetheless, he and Pethybridge pushed themselves hard, allowing only brief stops to refuel in Athens and Baghdad, before reaching Allahabad, 29½ hours out from England. Without pausing to sleep, they refuelled and were airborne within an hour, bound for Bangkok.

Lady Southern Cross never arrived. At some time in the early hours of 8 November, she plunged into the Andaman Sea somewhere off the Burmese coast, taking with her the most legendary of Australian aviators and his young protégé. Their bodies were lost; the only traces of the aircraft to be recovered were the starboard undercarriage and some metal fragments from the fuselage. The cause of the accident remains contentious among Australian aviation historians, most suggesting either a mechanical failure or Kingsford Smith's loss of consciousness in his ill and exhausted state. In any case, with his and Ulm's passing, the golden era of Australian aviation pioneers had finished.

The 'Sir Charles Kingsford Smith Memorial'

On 18 July 1935, when Kingsford Smith delivered the 'old bus' to the RAAF base at Richmond, near Sydney, the Minister for Defence announced, 'The *Southern Cross* now becomes the property of every Australian'. The government, he explained, would put the aircraft on display in Canberra as a national monument to Kingsford Smith and the remarkable era of aviation that he represented.

Nevertheless, for the next two decades few Australians had the opportunity to see *Southern Cross*. It would only make two brief public appearances in between spending years in storage sheds at Mascot and, for a brief time during the Second World War, at Fairbairn aerodrome in Canberra. In 1945 the film production company Cinesound convinced the RAAF to restore the aircraft to flying condition to appear in the feature film *Smithy*. Kingsford Smith and Ulm's old flying partner Bill Taylor flew *Southern Cross* in the film's airborne sequences. Two years later, in October 1947, the New South Wales branch of the Royal Aero Club secured permission to display 'the old bus' at its anniversary air pageant at Bankstown aerodrome. Then it went back into storage for another decade.

It was not until the mid-1950s that the government began to act on its 20-year-old promise to preserve *Southern Cross* as a permanent public monument. A committee headed by Liberal MP Bruce Wight raised funds by public subscription for what it dubbed the 'Sir Charles Kingsford Smith Memorial', a museum and interpretive centre to house *Southern Cross* at Brisbane airport, a few hundred metres from where it had landed at the end of the trans-Pacific flight. The committee planned to open the monument around the journey's 30th anniversary.

John Ulm, who at this time worked with the managing executive of Qantas, proposed finding Harry Lyon and Jim Warner and bringing them out to attend the ceremony. After flying the Pacific, both men had eked out comparatively quiet lives. Warner opened a radio repair business in San Francisco, but its failure during the Depression forced him to return to the life of a travelling salesman. He served in the United States Navy during the Second World War and was, in 1958, living in quiet retirement with his sixth wife in California, close to where the events that had briefly made him famous began. Lyon proved more difficult for Ulm to track down, but he eventually traced him to the small town of Paris Hill, in Maine. After the Pacific flight Lyon had returned to his family home there and over the next several years attempted to organise a number of flying adventures. None of them ever got off the ground. Aside from a stint in the Navy during the Second World War, his remained a small-town life and he finished his working days as the town's deputy sheriff.

William Dargie's 1961 painting Sir Charles Kingsford Smith and Captain Charles Ulm *evokes the optimism of the partnership's early days.*

There is no evidence that Lyon or Warner ever saw Kingsford Smith and Ulm after leaving Australia in June 1928.

John Ulm arranged for Warner, Lyon and their wives to retrace the 1928 flight, but this time in the comfort of a Qantas Super Constellation. With a film crew, they visited Oakland aerodrome, Wheeler Field, Suva and Naselai beach, before arriving in Brisbane in time for the unveiling of the Sir Charles Kingsford Smith Memorial. Surviving radio broadcasts reveal that the personalities of the two Americans had changed little in three decades. Warner retained the self-effacing, even shy demeanour that had caused him to always duck attention and publicity, while Lyon, still exuding wit and charisma, acted as the party's spokesperson, charming all he met. By all accounts, he still enjoyed a drink.

The Sir Kingsford Smith Memorial opened at Brisbane airport on a brilliantly sunny 17 August 1958. Around 500 invited guests and 3,000 spectators ('pilgrims', the press called them) witnessed an aerial display by air force fighter jets followed by an official address by the federal Treasurer, Sir Arthur Fadden. In the months leading up to the ceremony, dozens of people who had known Kingsford Smith and Ulm had written to the government, protesting the lack of recognition the memorial gave Southern Cross' original 'co-commander', Charles Ulm. Their lobbying didn't achieve a name change of the memorial but it resulted in a

plaque mentioning Ulm. In fact, during the official proceedings the only reference to Ulm's significance came, perhaps surprisingly, from Harry Lyon. 'Charlie Ulm was a great aviator any country would be proud to claim', he told the audience. 'This is Smithy's day, but he would be the last man in the world to begrudge mention of his co-pilot.'

John Ulm found Lyon's gesture moving; he still recalls it with a great deal of gratitude. Nonetheless, he has since found himself correcting official statements (including in one instance, by a prime minister) regarding his father's place in what is too often presented as the 'Smithy' story. In 1980 he was still corresponding with the Kingsford Smith Memorial Trust to secure his father a mention in their promotional and educational material.

In September 1957, Southern Cross went on display in Sydney's Hyde Park one last time before its final journey to Brisbane. For two shillings, people could inspect the aircraft up close, look through the windows and take home a pamphlet on its history. Dorothy Drain, editor of the Australian Women's Weekly, went and had a look. She was, frankly, underwhelmed by the tired-looking aircraft. Peering through the windows on the fuselage she made out 'the tiny shabby cabin' and a couple of 'battered, uncomfortable seats'. It didn't seem to match the rhetoric in the newspapers, which described the aircraft as a 'relic' that was to be 'enshrined' in Brisbane in front of thousands of 'pilgrims'.

Indeed, Drain—like many others—had good reason to find not much remarkable about *Southern Cross*. Its dull fabric covering, boxy appearance and sparse interior were a world away from the 'jet age' of the 1950s. Yet, as Drain suddenly realised, this was precisely where the aircraft's significance to future generations lay. *Southern Cross*, in its rough, unassuming plainness represented the extraordinarily rapid development of aviation in the twentieth century and the handful of remarkable, forward-thinking individuals like Charles Ulm and Charles Kingsford Smith who were wholly responsible for it; and, who lost their lives in pursuit of its development.

'You could see enough', Drain concluded after reflection. 'Enough to evoke Smithy and his crew aloft over the Pacific, enough to remind you of the wild adventure that was aviation nearly 30 years ago.'

Southern Cross on display at the Sir Charles Kingsford Smith Memorial, once again parked near where it landed on 9 June 1928.

'You could see enough … to evoke Smithy and his crew aloft over the Pacific.'

APPENDIX

Trans-Pacific flight statistics

First leg: California to Hawaii

Take-off: Oakland aerodrome, California, 8.54 am, Thursday, 31 May 1928

Landing: Wheeler Field, Oahu, 12.17 pm, Friday, 1 June 1928

Distance: 3,876 kilometres

Flying time: 27 hours 23 minutes

Average ground speed: 141.5 kilometres per hour

Second leg: Hawaii to Fiji

Take-off: Barking Sands, Kauai, 5.22 am, Sunday, 3 June 1928

Landing: Albert Park, Suva, 3.50 pm, Tuesday, 5 June 1928

Distance: 5,079 kilometres

Flying time: 34 hours 32 minutes

Average ground speed: 147 kilometres per hour

Third leg: Fiji to Australia

Take-off: Naselai, 2.52 pm, Friday, 8 June 1928

Landing: Eagle Farm aerodrome, Brisbane, 10.50 am, Saturday, 9 June 1928

Distance: 2,962 kilometres (including the detour via Ballina, New South Wales)

Flying time: 19 hours 58 minutes

Average ground speed: 148 kilometres per hour

Total flying time: 81 hours 53 minutes

Total distance: 11,917 kilometres

Overall average ground speed: 145.5 kilometres per hour

In addition to this, *Southern Cross* made an hour flight between Wheeler Field and Barking Sands and a 55-minute flight between Albert Park and Naselai.

Kingsford Smith estimated that each of the three propellers had made approximately 8 million revolutions during the flight.

ACKNOWLEDGEMENTS

Susan Hall, Publishing Manager at the National Library of Australia, commissioned this book in September 2010 after reading a review for my first book, the then recently published, *Fire in the Sky: The Australian Flying Corps in the First World War*. I'd like to thank her for having faith in a historian still in the early days of his career and for providing such efficient management of this project. Her encouragement, insight and criticism have all contributed to this book and are greatly appreciated.

I'd also like to acknowledge the professionalism and expertise of Susan's colleagues at the National Library, Senior Editor Jo Karmel and Image Content Coordinator Felicity Harmey. The Library assigned Maree Bentley to work on this project as a research assistant. Her diligent detective work turned up a number of valuable sources and made researching and writing a book while living outside Canberra much easier than it may have been otherwise. John Mapps edited the manuscript, providing it with a much-needed polish, and designer Liz Faul turned my black and white prose into the attractive volume before you.

Among the plethora of books on Kingsford Smith, Ian Mackersey's *Smithy: The Life of Sir Charles Kingsford Smith* remains the standard work. In preparing his compelling, eminently readable example of historical biography, Ian tracked down a number of Kingsford Smith's ex-colleagues and family members, many then in the twilight of their lives. Ian generously shared material he had obtained in the United States from the families of Jim Warner and Harry Lyon, allowing me to position Charles Ulm's log within a richer context of the crew's experiences of the flight.

The highlight of researching and writing this book has been meeting and striking up a friendship with Charles Ulm's son, John. He and his wife Valda extended me the warmest hospitality and John patiently weathered my barrage of questions. Though by his own admission, he has few memories of his father (and none preceding the trans-Pacific flight) his understanding of those times and insight into the personalities of his father's colleagues proved invaluable. Besides, it is not every day that a historian gets to have lunch with a man who flew Spitfires in combat during the Second World War and worked with the management of Qantas during its post-war transition into a truly global airline. This book is for John—son of a great Australian aviation pioneer and indeed, one in his own right.

Despite already knowing the cost of having a husband committed to writing a book, my wife Melissa encouraged this project from the outset and supported it with love, grace and patience—traits she displays in epic enough proportions (despite my failings) to be worthy of a book of their own.

Michael Molkentin
November 2011
www.michaelmolkentin.com

LIST OF ILLUSTRATIONS

Page 22
Charles Kingsford Smith and Charles Ulm in Aviation Suits 1929
black and white photograph; 30.5 x 17.1 cm
on mount 48.1 x 29.9 cm
Pictures Collection
nla.pic-vn3930973

Page 23
H.B. Miller
Harry Lyon, James Warner, Charles Kingsford Smith and Charles Ulm in front of the Southern Cross, Fokker Monoplane VH-USU, with Three Friends, before Take-off for Oakland from Los Angeles, California, Unites States 23 May 1928
black and white photograph; 20.7 x 25.5 cm
Pictures Collection
nla.pic-vn3930809

Page 24
The Southern Cross, Fokker Monoplane VH-USU Being Farewelled by Group of Onlookers, Long Beach Airport, Los Angeles, California, United States 23 May 1928
black and white photograph; 24.9 x 29.3 cm
Pictures Collection
nla.pic-vn4926307

Page 26
Map that appeared in newspaper in Captain Harry W. Lyon's personal papers
Manuscripts Collection
MS 5312

Page 27 (top)
East on 14th Street, San Leandro, California 1 October 1928
sepia-toned photograph
Courtesy Bancroft Library,
University of California, Berkeley

Page 27 (bottom)
North on Mission St from 29th St, San Francisco January 1928
Courtesy Bancroft Library, University of California, Berkeley

Page 28
Portrait of Charles Kingsford Smith and George Hubert Wilkins in front of the Southern Cross, Fokker Monoplane VH-USU, Oakland Aerodrome, California, United States 31 May 1928
black and white photograph; 36.1 x 49.5 cm
Pictures Collection
nla.pic-vn4926277

Page 29
Clock Belonging to Charles Kingsford Smith 1928
steel, 7.4 x 7.4 cm
Pictures Collection

Page 30
Group of Men at an Atlantic Union Oil Company Aircraft Refuelling Pump with Charles Ulm at the Pump c. 1928
sepia-toned photograph; 10.5 x 8.2 cm
Pictures Collection
nla.pic-vn3930639

Page 32
Unknown photographer
Portrait of Charles Ulm June 1928
black and white photograph; 21.7 x 16.5 cm
Pictures Collection
nla.pic-vn3930636

Page 33
Keystone View Company
Charles Kingsford Smith 1930
sepia-toned photograph; 20.7 x 16.4 cm
Pictures Collection
nla.pic-vn3424257

Page 35
Group of Adults and Children Standing next to the Wing of the Southern Cross, a Fokker F.VII/3m Monoplane, VH-USU, Looking up, Perhaps at an Aeroplane c. 1928
sepia-toned photograph; 8.5 x 10.5 cm
Pictures Collection
nla.pic-vn3930641

Page 40
US Navy Hydrographic Office
North Pacific Ocean Eastern Part
September 1927
part of *Navigational Charts Used by Charles Kingsford Smith in the 1928 Crossing of the Pacific*
Maps Collection
nla.map-rm2811-5

Page 42
Charles Ulm Servicing the Engine of the Southern Cross, a Fokker F.VII/3m Monoplane, G-AUSU c. 1928
sepia-toned photograph; 8.4 x 10.6 cm
Pictures Collection
nla.pic-vn3930643

Page 43
Sun Feature Bureau
Portrait of Radio Operator James Warner Testing the Wireless in the Southern Cross, Fokker Monoplane F.VII/3m, VH-USU 1928
black and white photograph; 10.5 x 16.5 cm
Pictures Collection
nla.pic-vn3930743

Page 45
H.B. Miller
Portrait of Harry Lyon, Charles Ulm, Charles Kingsford Smith and James Warner in front of the Southern Cross, a Fokker F.VII/3m Monoplane, VH-USU, Los Angeles, California, United States 23 May 1928
black and white photograph; 20.7 x 25.5 cm
Pictures Collection
nla.pic-vn3930681

Page 46
H.B. Miller
Cabin of Kingsford Smith's Fokker F.VII/3m Trimotor Monoplane, VH-USU, Southern Cross, Looking Forward towards the Cockpit, Showing Extra Fuel Tank, Brisbane, Queensland 1928
black and white photograph; 20.5 x 25.1 cm
Pictures Collection
nla.pic-vn4916633

Page 49
Charles Kingsford Smith in the Cockpit of Fokker Trimotor Monoplane VH-USU Southern Cross during Trans-Tasman flight 1928
black and white photograph; 16.0 x 20.6 cm
Norman Ellison Collection
nla.pic-vn4970358

Page 54
Sam Hood (1872–1953)
[Composite photograph of "Southern Cross" FH-USU in flight. Note exhaust pipes over the wings]
Courtesy State Library of New South Wales

Page 55
Kingsford Smith's World Flight 3 Shilling Postage Stamp 1931
Courtesy National Archives of Australia
A1200/18

Page 87
Charles Ulm
Hand Drawn Map of Enderbury Island 1928
pencil on paper
The Charles TP Ulm Collection of
historical aviation records, Part 1, 1919–
1965: MLMSS 3359
Courtesy State Library of New South Wales

Page 88
Thomas Harris, London
Nautical Sextant 190–?
brass; 11.5 x 30.5 x 25.5 cm in box
Pictures Collection
nla.pic-an6227519

Page 89
Map that appeared in newspaper in Captain
Harry W. Lyon's personal papers
Manuscripts Collection
MS 5312

Page 90
Heintz and Kaufman, San Francisco
Southern Cross' Radio Receiver c. 1927
aluminium; 31 x 64.7 x 15.4 cm
Pictures Collection
nla.pic-an876346

Page 93
US Coast and Geodetic Survey
Territory of Hawaii 1925
part of *Navigational Charts Used by Charles
Kingsford Smith in the 1928 Crossing of the Pacific*
Maps Collection
nla.map-rm2811-3

Page 95
Associated Newspapers
*The Southern Cross, Fokker F. VII/3m Monoplane,
VH-USU Being Greeted by Fijians, Albert Park,
Suva* 5 June 1928
black and white photograph; 19.3 x 24.8 cm
Pictures Collection
nla.pic-vn3930686

Page 100
Ernest Crome (1902–1987)
*A Representation of the Southern Cross Over the
Water* c. 1958
oil on composition board; 20 x 25.3 cm
Pictures Collection
nla.pic-an2288394

Page 103
Auckland Weekly News
*The Fokker Tri-motor Monoplane, Southern Cross
(VH-USU) at Mt Egmont, New Zealand* c. 1933
sepia-toned photograph; 16.5 x 20.8 cm
Pictures Collection
nla.pic-vn3722918

Page 104
Green and Hahn, Christchurch
*Charles Kingsford Smith in the Cockpit of the Southern
Cross, VH-USU, during Trans-Tasman Flight* 1928
black and white photograph; 20.7 x 15.7 cm
Pictures Collection
nla.pic-vn3723611

Page 106
United States Hydrographic Office
*Navigation Chart Used by Sir Charles Kingsford
Smith in the 1928 Crossing of the Pacific* 1902–25
one of seven maps; 118 x 95.5 cm or smaller
Maps Collection
nla.map-rm2811-4

Page 107
Southern Cross at Richmond, New South Wales 1928
black and white photograph; 10.8 x 16.8 cm
Fred Morton Collection
nla.pic-vn4690364

Page 109
*The Southern Cross, a Fokker F.VII/3m Monoplane,
VH-USU Landing at Albert Park, Suva*
5 June 1928
black and white photograph; 8.6 x 10.9 cm
Pictures Collection
nla.pic-vn3930687

Page 111
*Portrait of Charles Kingsford Smith, Charles Ulm
and T.H. McWilliam at Beer Garden, Great Pacific
Hotel, Suva* 1928
black and white photograph; 8.5 x 13.7 cm
Pictures Collection
nla.pic-vn3930659

Page 114
*The Southern Cross, a Fokker Monoplane F.VII/3m,
VH-USU, Guarded by British Troops, Being Greeted
by the Crowd, Albert Park, Suva, Fiji* 5 June 1928
black and white photograph; 16.9 x 21.8 cm
Pictures Collection
nla.pic-vn3930692

Page 115
*Locals Crowd behind a Rope Cordon Waiting for
Charles Kingsford Smith to Land, Fiji* June 1928
black and white photograph; 6.6 x 11.2 cm
Ann Bernard Album
nla.pic-vn4938063

Page 116
*Portrait of the Mayor of Suva, Mr Marks, and
Charles Kingsford Smith, Fijian chief and Harry
Lyon with Unidentified Men in the Background,
Suva, Fiji* 7 June 1928
sepia-toned postcard; 8.8 x 14 cm
Pictures Collection
nla.pic-vn3930702

Page 117 (top)
*A 1918 Australian Florin, which together with
a Fijian Five Shilling Note Was Enclosed in an
Australian National Airways Envelope Belonging to
Charles Ulm* 1918–25
coin: silver; diameter 2.8 cm
Pictures Collection
nla.pic-vn3945041

Page 117 (middle)
*Crowd next to the Southern Cross, a Fokker F.VII/3m
Monoplane, VH-USU, Albert Park, Suva, Fiji*
5 June 1928
black and white photograph; 8.5 x 13.9 cm
Pictures Collection
nla.pic-vn3930695

Page 117 (bottom)
*Guard Clearing Crowd before Departure of the
Southern Cross, a Fokker F.VII/3m Monoplane,
VH-USU, from Albert Park, Suva* June 1928
sepia-toned photograph; 16.8 x 21.8 cm
Pictures Collection
nla.pic-vn3930699

Page 148 (middle)
Unknown photographer
Landing the Aircraft, Southern Cross, in Brisbane, Queensland c. 1928
black and white photograph
Courtesy State Library of Queensland

Page 148 (bottom)
Cliff Postle (1913-2004)
Crowds Welcome the Southern Cross with Crew at Eagle Farm, Queensland 9 June 1928
black and white digital print; 13.9 x 25 cm
Pictures Collection
nla.pic-vn4929587

Page 149
Charles Ulm Leaving his Cockpit at Brisbane September 1928
black and white photograph; 16.6 x 21.6 cm
Pictures Collection
nla.pic-vn3583053

Page 150
Relaxed Portrait of Sir Charles Kingsford Smith on Arrival in Brisbane in 1928 after His Record-breaking Flight 1928
black and white photoprint
Courtesy State Library of Queensland

Page 151 (top)
The Sun Feature Bureau
Crew of the Southern Cross, Fokker Monoplane VH-USU, Leaving the Airport with Police Escort, Surrounded by the Crowd, Brisbane 9 June 1928
black and white photograph; 10.5 x 15.8 cm
Pictures Collection
nla.pic-vn3930716

Page 151 (bottom)
The Sun Feature Bureau
Crew of the Southern Cross, a Fokker F.VII/3m Monoplane, VH-USU Being Driven through Crowds in the Streets of Brisbane 9 June 1928
black and white photograph; 10.8 x 15.9 cm
Pictures Collection
nla.pic-vn3930719

Page 152
Sydney Morning Herald and Sydney Mail
Charles Kingsford Smith with Charles Ulm Taken just after the Trans-Pacific flight 1928
black and white photograph; 11.3 x 16.0 cm
Pictures Collection
nla.pic-an24111366

Page 153
Crew of the Southern Cross, Fokker Monoplane VH-USU, Being Farewelled by Two Unidentified Men in Car and by Other Well-Wishers, Eagle Farm Aerodrome 10 June 1928
black and white photograph; 16.6 x 21.6 cm
Pictures Collection
nla.pic-vn3930717

page 154
Milton Kent
Aerial View of Sydney, Showing Early Construction Stage of Harbour Bridge, Circular Quay, City Centre and Bennelong Point 10 June 1928
black and white photograph
Pictures Collection
nla.pic-vn3930722

Page 155
The Sun Feature Bureau
Aerial View of Mascot Aerodrome and Surrounding Market Gardens, with the Southern Cross, a Fokker Monoplane F.VII/3m, VH-USU on the Ground Surrounded by a Crowd, at the End of the First Trans-Pacific Flight, Sydney 10 June 1928
black and white photograph; 17.5 x 24.6 cm
Pictures Collection
nla.pic-vn3930726

Page 157
Broughton Ward & Chaseling, Sydney
The Southern Cross on its Arrival in Sydney from the Flight across the Pacific 10 June 1928
black and white photograph; 30.9 x 38.6 cm
Pictures Collection
nla.pic-an24664462

Page 158 (top)
Crew of the Southern Cross, Fokker Monoplane VH-USU on Dais Surrounded by Photographers and Welcoming Crowd, Mascot Aerodrome, Sydney 10 June 1928
black and white photograph; 27.1 x 34.4 cm
Pictures Collection
nla.pic-vn3930975

Page 158 (bottom)
The Sun Feature Bureau
James Warner Starting the Starboard Motor of the Southern Cross, Fokker Monoplane F.VII/3m, VH-USU, before Takeoff to Melbourne from Sydney 10 June 1928
sepia-toned photograph; 10.5 x 16.7 cm
Pictures Collection
nla.pic-vn3930739

Page 159
Unknown photographer
Kingsford Smith's Parents
black and white photograph
part of the Hood Collection part II
[Aviation]
Courtesy State Library of New South Wales

Page 160
James Warner, Charles Kingsford Smith, Harry Lyon and Charles Ulm with Aviation Plans and World Globe, Melbourne 1928
black and white photograph; 25.1 x 33.2 cm
Pictures Collection
nla.pic-vn4926217

Page 163 (top)
Unknown photographer
Farewell to Harry Lyon and Jim Warner
black and white photograph
Courtesy State Library of New South Wales

Page 163 (bottom)
Unknown photographer
Crowd Farewelling Lyon and Warner
black and white photograph
Courtesy State Library of New South Wales

Page 165
J.T. Harrison
Staff of Australian National Airways Posing in front of Hangar c. 1929
black and white photograph; 15.2 x 20.2 cm
Pictures Collection
nla.pic-vn4197936

Page 170
Smithy and Charles Jnr c. 1930
sepia-toned photograph; 14.6 x 9.3 cm
Pictures Collection
nla.pic-vn3723609

Page 172
Hall & Co., Sydney
Southern Cross Flying over the Sydney Harbour Bridge 1931
gelatin silver toned photograph; 32 x 25.5 cm
Pictures Collection
nla.pic-an6820583

BIBLIOGRAPHY

Listed below are the publications and collections consulted in researching this book. For detailed references visit www.michaelmolkentin.com.

Archival sources

National Library of Australia, Canberra

Austin Byrne, Papers of Austin Byrne, 1932–1993, MS 3736

Ernest and Virtie Crome, Papers of Ernest and Virtie Crome, 1784–2005, MS 1925

Norman Ellison, Papers of Norman Ellison, circa 1900–1971, MS 1882

Charles Kingsford Smith and Charles Ulm, Interview with Kingsford Smith and Ulm, 1928, for 2BL radio, ORAL TRC 39/2

Charles Kingsford Smith, Internal NLA correspondence regarding acquisition of Kingsford Smith's papers, TRIM file 202/04/00111

Charles Kingsford Smith, Navigation charts used by Sir Charles Kingsford Smith…, MAP RM 2811

Charles Kingsford Smith, Papers of Charles Kingsford Smith, 1917–1935, MS 209

Charles Kingsford Smith, Papers of Charles Kingsford Smith, 1921–1929, MS 5918

Henry Lyon and James Warner, Interview with Henry Lyon and James Warner, 1958, for 2GB radio, ORAL TRC 22/4

Charles and John Ulm, Papers of Charles and John Ulm, 1803–2010 MS 9923

National Archives of Australia, Canberra and Melbourne

Aircraft history file – VH-USU – S/N-SCA-28. Make – Fokker, model – F-VIIB/3M "Southern Cross", J778 VH-USU Part 1

Aircraft history file – VH-USU – S/N-SCA-28. Make – Fokker, model – F-VIIB/3M "Southern Cross", J778 VH-USU Part 2

Kingsford Smith flight from San Francisco & Australia and Australia to New Zealand, MP124/6 415/201/406

Purchase of Monoplane 'Southern Cross' from Sir Charles Kingsford Smith, A432 1935/1295

Sir C. Kingsford Smith Pacific flights proposed flight USA to Australia, A705 21/1/61 Part 1

Sir C. Kingsford Smith Pacific flights USA to Australia 1928, A705 21/1/61 Part 2

State Library of New South Wales, Sydney

Charles Ulm, Charles Thomas Phillippe Ulm papers, 1927–1934, with miscellaneous papers of Mary Josephine Ulm, 1928–1935, MLMSS 2209

Charles Ulm, Charles Ulm – photographs and albums, 1928–1934, PXD 921

Charles Ulm, The Charles T.P. Ulm collection of historical aviation records, Parts 1 and 2, 1919–1987, MLMSS 3359

Ian Mackersey Papers (privately held), Auckland

Charles M. Hodge, log of radio messages received from *Southern Cross*

Henry Lyon, manuscript memoir, no date

James W. Warner, 'The trans-Pacific flight', manuscript memoir, c. 1929

Published sources

Bob Boulton, *Aviators of the Charles Ulm and Charles Kingsford Smith Era*. Sydney: Echidna Publishing, 1993.

Stanley Brogden, *The History of Australian Aviation*. London: The Hawthorne Press, 1960.

Pedr Davis, *Charles Kingsford Smith: The World's Greatest Aviator*. Sydney: Summit Books, 1977.

Norman Ellison, *Flying Matilda: Early Days of Australian Aviation*. Sydney: Angus & Robertson, 1957.

Peter FitzSimons, *Charles Kingsford Smith and Those Magnificent Men*. Sydney: HarperCollins, 2009.

Lloyd S. Gates, 'Harry Lyon and the *Southern Cross*', *American Aviation Historical Society Journal*, vol. 24, no. 4, Winter 1979.

Ralph M. Heintz, 'How the Americans Described the *Southern Cross* Flight', *Popular Hobbies*, vol. IV, no. 3, August 1928.

Ralph M. Heintz, 'Southern Cross: A Radio Victory', *Popular Mechanics*, August 1928.

Charles Kingsford Smith, *My Flying Life: An Authentic Biography Prepared Under the Personal Supervision of and from the Diaries and Papers of the Late Sir Charles Kingsford-Smith*. London: Andrew Melrose, 1937.

C. E. Kingsford Smith and C. T. P. Ulm, *Story of "Southern Cross" Trans-Pacific Flight 1928*. Sydney: Penlington & Somerville, 1928.

Charles Kingsford Smith and Charles Ulm, 'Our Conquest of the Pacific', *The National Geographic Magazine*, vol. LIV, no. 4, October 1928.

Ian Mackersey, Smithy: *The Life of Charles Kingsford Smith*. London: Warner Books, 1999.

Ward McNally, *The Man on the Twenty Dollar Note*. Sydney: A.H. and A.W. Reed, 1976.

Neville Parnell and Trevor Boughton, *Flypast: A Record of Aviation in Australia*. Canberra: Australian Government Publishing Service, 1988.

Ellen Rogers, *Faith in Australia: Charles Ulm and Australian Aviation*. Crows Nest: Book Production Services, 1987.

Beau Sheil, *Caesar of the Skies*. London: Cassell, 1937.

James W. Warner and John Robert Johnson, 'The Trans-Pacific Flight', *Liberty*, 19 April 1930.

Richard Williams, *These Are Facts: The Autobiography of Air Marshal Sir Richard Williams*. Canberra: Australian War Memorial and Australian Government Printing Service, 1977.

Newspapers

The Argus (Melbourne)

The Barrier Miner (Broken Hill)

The Canberra Times

The Courier Mail (Brisbane)

The Daily Telegraph (Sydney)

The Guardian (Sydney)

The LA Examiner

Mercury (Hobart)

The New York Times

The Sun

The Sydney Morning Herald

Cartoon by Tom Glover that appeared in a newspaper in Captain Harry W. Lyon's personal papers; Manuscripts Collection, MS 5312

INDEX

Note: Bold page numbers refer to illustrations